THE FRENCH
HOW THEY LIVE AND WORK

The French

HOW THEY LIVE AND WORK

Joseph T. Carroll

DAVID & CHARLES : NEWTON ABBOT

7153 4244 4

First published 1968 by David & Charles Limited
South Devon House · Railway Station · Newton Abbot · Devon

Revised edition 1970

Copyright © Joseph T. Carroll 1968, 1970

Printed in Great Britain by
Redwood Press Limited
London and Trowbridge

Contents

Contents

Note
Figures given in dollars are based on the exchange rate current in 1969 prior to the devaluation of the franc in August of that year (see page 66).
Figures given in pounds are based on the exchange rate established by the sterling devaluation on 18 November 1967 except where they are stated specifically to refer to the preceding period, eg total revenue on page 67 is for the year 1965 and is calculated at the pre-devaluation rate but the estimates of Paris rents on page 74 are based on the new exchange rate.
The British reader is reminded that 'billion', in sums of dollars, is used in the American sense, ie meaning 1,000 million.

List of Illustrations

ACKNOWLEDGMENTS

I wish to express my thanks to the following for the use of their photographs : Commissariat General au Tourisme : Page 17 : above (Feuillie), below (Viguier); Page 18 : above (Feuillie), below; Page 35 : left (Marton), right (Haury); Page 36 : (Marton); Page 53 : left (Marton), right; Page 54 : above (Delvert); Page 71 : left (Feher), right (Marton); Page 90 : (Poinot); Page 107 : above (Feuillie), Page 125 : (Guillemaut); EDF Service Creation-Diffusion : Page 54 : below (Baranger); Page 108 : (Brigaud); Photo Esso : Page 72; Page 107 : below; Photo S.N.C.F. Page 89 : above; Photo Societe Bertin : Page 89 : below; Documentation Française : Page 126 : above (Bommer); Institut Pedagogique National : Page 126 : below (Suquet); Page 144 : (Allard); Ministère des Affaires Etrangères : Page 143.

To my mother

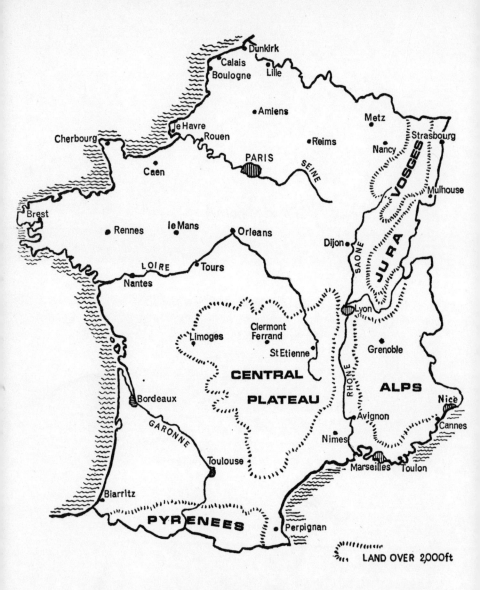

Detailed relief maps of France and its regions can be obtained
from the Institut Géographique National at 107 Rue la Boétie,
Paris 8e.

Maps showing the implantation of industries and agriculture
can be obtained from the Société d'Editions Géographiques
Professionnelles at 9 Rue Coetlogon, Paris 6e.

I

The Country and the People

THE originality of France, geographically speaking, is to sum up in one country the principal physical characteristics of the European continent. Her position on the western end of the European land-mass has ensured for France a dual destiny as a continental and a maritime power with coastal boundaries of the Atlantic, the Mediterranean and the English Channel matched by land frontiers formed by the Alps, Pyrenees and part of the Rhine. Only in the north-east, where she faces Germany and Belgium, does France lack a clear-cut 'natural frontier,' and to this fact is due much of her troubled history of successive invasions.

Within her ample boundaries France contains an astonishing diversity of physical features, all of which substantiate her claim to be a Europe in miniature. The very size of France is impressive by European standards. The land area of the French mainland and the island of Corsica, totalling 213,000 square miles, is bigger than any other country in Europe with the exception of Russia and is more than double that of England, Scotland and Wales (89,000 square miles).

Basically the country consists of three great river basins, the Paris basin, drained by the Somme, Seine and Loire, the Rhône-Saône basin and the Garonne basin which lie respectively north, east and south-west of the block of mountains known as the Central Plateau, in which some of the old volcanic peaks called *puys* rise to over 6,000 feet.

The narrow Rhône valley which cuts a trough between the steep eastern flanks of the Central Plateau and the lower slopes of the Alps is well known to tourists as providing the principal means of access between the northern plains and the Mediterranean coast. The famous *Route Nationale 7* which holiday-makers drive down, along the left bank of the Rhône on the way to the sunny *Midi*, the *Côte d'Azur* and the Italian Riviera is the same road which the Roman legionaries took, only going in the opposite direction, when they conquered all Gaul for Caesar.

Another famous route from the Mediterranean passes from the region called Languedoc, west of the mouth of the Rhône, through the Gate of Carcassonne which separates the south-eastern tip of the Central Plateau from the Pyrenees. Once through this narrow pass the traveller is in the fertile region of the Garonne basin known as Aquitaine, once ruled over by English kings. Another link with Britain is the wine trade which for centuries has passed through the port of Bordeaux and has made British palates familiar with the clarets and cognacs for which the region is famous.

These lowlands, which stretch from the Central Plateau westwards to the Bay of Biscay, merge at their northern extremity into the extensive Paris basin. This region, which covers most of the northern half of the country, is a prolongation of the Great European Plain which enters France through the Flanders plain in the north-east. It occupies the depression bounded by the older rock formations of the Brittany peninsula on the west, the Ardennes on the east and the Central Plateau on the south; the sedimentary limestone rocks of the floor of the basin form a series of concentric rings suggesting a nest of saucers with the successive edges standing out as scarps.

Much of the region around the capital itself, known as the *Ile de France*, is still forested, a reminder of the time when the dukes and later the kings of France hunted there. From time to time important visiting statesmen are still invited to shoots in the presidential demesne at Rambouillet, south-west of Paris on the way to Chartres. The twin spires of the twelfth century cathedral at Chartres, seen from a certain angle, seem to rise dramatically out of the rolling wheatfields of the plain called the Beauce which is one of the most fertile in France thanks to the rich limestone soil.

The site of Paris itself on the Seine was originally dictated by defensive reasons, as the Gaulish tribe the *Parisii* founded the city on a small island, still called today the *Cité*, on a bend in the river between the points where it is joined by the tributaries of the Marne and the Oise. The position of Paris in the middle of the northern plain allowed it to exercise a strong centralising influence which the passage of time and revolutionary upheavals have only increased.

To the north of the capital the road to the Channel coast passes over the low chalk hills of Picardy, drained by the Somme and scene of bitter fighting in both world wars. To the east the road which follows the Marne, known cynically as the ' invasion route,' traverses the Champagne plateau, home of the sparkling wine, until the plains are broken by the foothills of Lorraine and the higher forested slopes of the Vosges where the major peaks called *ballons* rise to 4,000 feet. On the eastern side of the range is the vulnerable province of Alsace lying in the narrow rift valley formed by the Rhine and facing the Black Forest across the river.

Directly south of the Vosges lie the Jura mountains which form the north-east outcrop of the Alps. The two ranges are separated by the historically important pass called the Gate of Burgundy or Belfort. This was the way into France taken by the Burgundian tribes who settled in the *Côte d'Or* region around Dijon, and whose early warlike tendencies were diverted to growing the vines which produce some of the greatest wines of France.

The rest of France's eastern frontier from Geneva to the Mediterranean is the majestic barrier of the Alps, dominated by Mont Blanc (15,782 feet), but no longer the hindrance they used to be to travellers since man learned how to bore holes in them. The seven-and-a-quarter-mile Mont Blanc road tunnel between Chamonix on the French side and Courmayeur on the Italian side, opened in 1965, was used by a million vehicles by March 1967 and plans are well advanced for two more road tunnels further south. The first, under the Fréjus col, would run parallel to the existing Mount Cenis rail tunnel linking Lyons and Grenoble with Turin, and the second would pierce the Maritime Alps under the Mercantour and considerably shorten the journey between Nice and Turin.

In obvious contrast to the long land frontier on the east, running for more than 1,000 miles, is the varied Atlantic seaboard on the west, stretching from the old rocks of the Brittany peninsula in the north past the mouth of the Loire, the deep estuary of the Gironde and the 140-mile strip of sand dunes south of Bordeaux which fringe the wild region of forest and marshes called the Landes, finishing at the Spanish frontier at Hendaye.

Before finishing this brief sketch of France's physical features it is worth while drawing attention to their remarkable symmetry and harmony. One of the first things a French child learns in geography class is how closely the outline of his country approximates to a hexagon. When drawing a map he is shown how to mark the six corners first and then join them up with dotted lines.

The proportions of the hexagon are impressively tidy in a way that appeals to the French taste for balance and harmony. The three coastal sides are matched by the three land frontiers and are almost equal in length, 1,760 miles and 1,665 miles. The lines joining the points furthest apart, running from Dunkirk in the north to Port Vendres on the Spanish border and from Ushant in Brittany to Strasbourg on the Rhine, are approximately 600 miles long and intersect satisfactorily at Paris which in turn is 420 miles distant from both the south-west and south-east corners.

This notion of the hexagon is one which stays with a Frenchman for life. In the days of the French Empire it was a colourful way of distinguishing the population of metropolitan France from those overseas, and even during the Algerian war the French settlers on the other side of the Mediterranean used to refer scornfully to their brethren in France as *les hexagones.* More recently, for the legislative election in 1967, the Gaullist party adopted a stylised hexagon for its symbol.

Although France's richest natural resources are primarily her fertile farm lands, forests and rivers, giving her an enviable self-sufficiency and a reputation as the granary of Europe, there are other substantial forms of wealth yielded from the ground.

Lorraine has the biggest reserves of iron ore in Europe and fifty-five million tons were mined in 1966. For the production of pig iron and steel France is also among the world's leaders. Coal is found principally on the Belgian border and in small scattered seams among the old rocks of the Central Plateau at places like Le Creusot-Blanzy and St Etienne. About fifty-two million tons were mined in 1966.

Bauxite is mined in large quantities in the southern department of the Var. More recent discoveries were oil in the Landes in the south-west and natural gas and sulphur at Lacq in the Pyrenees. Almost two million tons of potash salts were mined in 1964. Hydro-electric power is produced abundantly by alpine barrages and the fast-flowing Rhône, but the most spectacular achievement was the completion in 1967 of the tidal power generating station across the Rance estuary in Brittany.

CLIMATE

Like everything else in France the climate is extremely varied. It is the only country in which are represented the three European climatic subdivisions of continental, maritime and Mediterranean. Generally speaking the lower northern half of the country is less affected by the extremes of temperature and rainfall associated with the highland regions in the south; nevertheless no part has less than twenty inches of rain annually.

The wettest parts are the Central Plateau, the Jura, the Alps and the Pyrenees and on the north-west and west coasts around the Cherbourg peninsula, Brittany and the Landes. The heaviest rains are usually in the autumn.

The driest regions are the centre of the Paris basin and, of course, the Mediterranean coast, although local storms can cause torrential downpours in midsummer on the Riviera. The varied nature of the topography gives rise however to the phenomenon called a 'micro-climate,' whereby a minute area in the mountains or on the coast frequently escapes belts of general rain sweeping over the region. This is the case with some of the well-known holiday resorts in Brittany and the west coast and each summer there are complaints from hotel owners and others in the tourist trade that regional weather bulletins given by the radio and television services are consistently inaccurate and scare away holidaymakers.

In August 1966, the mayor of Biarritz asked that the television weather chart stop showing a cloud mass over the region because no rain had fallen for ten days. An angry telegram from a senator in the Pyrenees demanded the end of such 'meteorological fantasies.'

Temperatures in France are usually similar to those in Britain, but in summer the southern region or Midi can be extremely hot, especially along the coast where olives, oranges,

———

France is often called the country of a hundred cathedrals, two hundred families and three hundred cheeses. The cathedral of Chartres, built in the twelfth and thirteenth centuries, is one of the most magnificent examples in Europe of the Gothic-style architecture. The mysterious two hundred families refer to the financial domination once exercised by the two hundred biggest shareholders in the Bank of France and which was ended by the Popular Front Government in 1936. But the three hundred cheeses still play an important role in the country's gastronomical activities.

The Mont Blanc massif and the valley of Chamonix, forming the frontier between France, Switzerland and Italy, is one of the most recent acquisitions of France. It dates only from 1860 when Savoy became French.

mulberry and exotic vegetation such as palms, eucalyptus and acacias flourish in the sub-tropical temperatures.

A distinctive feature of the region is the cold wind known as the Mistral which blows down the Rhône valley carrying the cold air from the Alps and the Cevennes. Its full force is felt in the lowlands around the mouth of the Rhône in spring and autumn and barriers of cypress trees and reeds are planted to protect plants and crops.

RACIAL DERIVATION

France's unique position on the western edge of the continental land mass, exposed to Atlantic, Mediterranean and North Sea influences and easily accessible on her landward side to successive waves of immigration from the east, has destined her to be the melting-pot of a host of racial groups. The Frenchman of today has undoubtedly one of the most complicated ancestries in the world.

His origins go back far into the prehistoric era when, between successive ice ages, a race of hunters inhabited the limestone caves of the Dordogne region in the Central Plateau. The hunting scenes drawn on the walls of their caves by these Stone Age men

----

Two Paris squares intimately associated with the history of France. The Place des Vosges was built at the inspiration of Henri IV in 1605. Known then as the Place Royale, it immediately became the most fashionable part of Paris under Louis XIII. The nobles even duelled there until Cardinal Richelieu, who lived in Number 21, executed two of them who had the effrontery to defy his ban and fight under his window. Two hundred years later Victor Hugo lived in Number 6 which is preserved today as a museum.

The splendid Place de la Concorde was begun in 1755 under Louis XV and was at first named after him. His successor Louis XVI was guillotined there, as were most of the victims of the Reign of Terror. The Egyptian Obelisk in the centre is the oldest monument in Paris—thirty-three centuries.

are still preserved at Lascaux, although they were closed to the general public several years ago to prevent further deterioration. Anthropologists have observed that the present day inhabitants of the Dordogne reveal traces of descent from these prehistoric people.

After the retreat of the ice cap and the resultant warming-up of the climate the northward push of late Stone Age peoples from Africa gradually reached France with the race usually described as Mediterranean. They were distinguished by their short stature, oval face, longish head shape and dark hair, eyes and skin.

From the east was spreading a farming type of people who followed the central European mountain chains into France, hence the term Alpine race which is used today to describe them. Characterised by broad heads, they tended to be heavily built and short. They spread across France to the Central Plateau and the Atlantic coast. Their aptitude for farming and hard work has revealed itself in the French peasantry through the ages.

Then at a later stage the Nordic peoples, distinguished by their tall stature, blond colouring and blue or grey eyes, came out of Asia and advanced across northern Europe into the Paris basin. The early Celtic invaders belonged to this type which also penetrated into Britain and Ireland. Thus in the prehistoric era France was already being peopled by a mingling of races of the most varied character.

Some of the most interesting relics of these prehistoric settlers are to be found in Brittany. This westerly region, facing the Atlantic, was the end of the road for invasions by both land and sea routes, and in the early Bronze Age there was a remarkable period of building of great stone monuments, generally to mark burial sites. The life of Bretons today, especially in the Morbihan, still seems to bear traces of the magic druidic rites belonging to that far-off time.

To the south the first impact of Greek colonisation reached France with the founding of *Massalia*, now known as Marseilles, in about 600 BC. The new arrivals from the eastern Mediterranean probably introduced the cultivation of the vine and the olive and revealed to the primitive tribes scattered around the lower Rhône valley the refinements and graces of city life. The Greek influence, although concentrated along the coast at settlements which today have become Antibes and Nice, spread up the Rhône valley over the *Côte d'Or* hills as far as Champagne.

The Greeks were followed by the Romans who by the second century BC had established a province along the Mediterranean coast and inland as far as Toulouse and Vienne. The signs of this Roman influence are still to be seen today, notably in the well-preserved amphitheatres at Nîmes and Arles, the aqueduct of the Pont du Gard and the theatre at Orange. The region still keeps the name *Provence*.

Roman rule was extended to the whole country by Caesar's defeat of the Celtic Gauls (57-52 BC) but the Gaul divided into three parts which he describes in his Commentaries included the territory today occupied by Belgium, part of Holland and the Rhineland. In the northern *Belgica* and central *Celtica* the tribes spoke Celtic, but in the south-west region called *Aquitania* the Basque tongue, still heard in the Pyrenees and northern Spain, was probably spoken.

The Roman conquest of Gaul had a deeper and more lasting effect than that of Britain. This was especially so in the southern half of France because the area's climatical affinities with Italy and its earlier colonisation allowed Roman laws, customs and language to become firmly rooted. In the north, Roman rule found expression mainly in military occupation and the towns grew up around garrisons and at the intersections of the great roads with which the invaders criss-crossed the country. These early differences between north and south have persisted until modern times and we shall note examples of them when discussing language, laws, administration and national characteristics.

The barbarian invasions which battered France in the fifth century AD resulted in the widespread settlement all over the country of tribes of Central European origin speaking mainly Germanic dialects. The chief ones were Vandals, Visigoths, Franks, Burgundians and Alamans.

The geographical settlement of these fighting tribes played an important role in the subsequent history of France. The Visigoth empire extended from southern Spain as far north as the Loire and its influence was especially strong along the Mediterranean coast between the Pyrenees and the Rhône. The Burgundians, as we have seen, came into France through the Gate of Belfort and established themselves along the valleys of the Rhône and the Saône while the Franks settled in two groups in the north.

In time the Franks and their ruling house came to dominate the country from whence came its later name France from *Francia*, but before passing to a review of the principal historical landmarks let us finish tracing this extraordinary mixing of racial strains which lies behind the civilised figure of the Frenchman of today.

While the Franks were fighting to establish their control in northern France, the Angles and the Saxons were invading England and forcing the Celtic-speaking Britons to flee to Wales or across the English Channel to the Celts in Brittany, then known in the Celtic tongue as *Armor*, the country of the sea. It was from these Briton immigrants that the peninsula got its present-day name of *Bretagne*, the United Kingdom being called *Grande Bretagne*.

In the ninth century yet another wave of invaders arrived in France, the Norsemen who sailed up the Seine and attacked Paris in 886. Soon afterwards their chief, Rollo, was allowed by the Franks to settle in the area around the lower reaches of the Seine, known today as Normandy. It was a successor of Rollo called William who, 150 years later, led the Norman invasion fleet across the Channel and made England a colony, not of the kingdom of France which was still limited to the area around Paris, but of the powerful duchy of Normandy.

France was to know many subsequent invasions, but the Normans were the last settlers until the peaceful immigrations of the twentieth century when hundreds of thousands of foreign workers arrived to augment the falling population.

CHIEF HISTORICAL LANDMARKS

The divisions of Gaul which Caesar noted were only made

more widespread when the territory was overrun by the barbarian invaders, and for the next thousand years the energies
of successive rulers had to be devoted primarily to the attempt
to create a lasting national unity out of the disparate parts.
When Louis XIV succeeded to the throne in the seventeenth
century national unity had been achieved, although it needed
some further consolidation, so French ambitions turned outwards
in search of the leading role among European nations.

The defeat of Napoleon at Waterloo 170 years later ended
this expansionist phase and thereafter France was forced to concentrate on defending herself from the territorial ambitions of her
neighbour across the Rhine. Outside Europe her soldiers, administrators and missionaries in the latter half of the nineteenth
century built up a vast empire, mainly in Africa.

In the meantime had taken place that astonishing internal
upheaval which shocked the world, known as the French
Revolution, whose effects are still working themselves out in the
France of the 1970s. We shall now look briefly at the principal
landmarks in this historical process.

The Treaty of Verdun (843) which divided up Charlemagne's
Holy Roman Empire between his three grandsons marks the
beginning of France as a separate kingdom. Louis received the
German territories east of the Rhine, Lothair a narrow strip
comprising the valleys of the Meuse, Rhône and Saône in
addition to Italy and the title of Emperor, and Charles the
Bald became King of the Franks with a nominal control over
the rest of Gaul.

In practice the king's rule was confined to the small area
around Paris called the *Ile de France*, and under the disintegrat-
ing influence of the feudal system the rest of the country
gradually became a series of powerful independent duchies such
as Brittany, Flanders, Toulouse, Gascony, Aquitaine, Provence
and Burgundy.

The accession to the throne of Hugh Capet in 987 was the
beginning of the long process of winning over the autonomous
provinces, duchies and counties to allegiance to the French
crown which went on until the end of the fifteenth century. The

Capetian line marked a break with the Carolingian system of dividing up the kingdom among the male heirs, and all the subsequent kings of France down to the last, Louis-Philippe, are descended from Hugh Capet. The present Count of Paris, Henri d'Orleans, is known as the Pretender to the throne because of his direct descent from Louis-Philippe.

The English foothold in France established by descendants of William the Conqueror over large regions of the south-west was broken by the Hundred Years War (1337-1453), and the Bourbon monarchy, a branch of the Capetians, who succeeded in the person of Henry IV in 1589, initiated the push towards France's natural frontiers.' Under Louis XIII and Louis XIV this aim was largely achieved thanks to the diplomatic genius of their prime ministers Cardinal Richelieu and Cardinal Mazarin, and by 1678 the French borders in the south-west, east and north-east lay along the Pyrenees, the Rhine and the Ardennes.

Louis XIV feared the threat to national unity posed by the Protestant Huguenots who had been guaranteed religious freedom by the Edict of Nantes (1598). The revocation of the edict in 1685 drove large numbers of the talented and industrious Protestants into exile, imposing a religious uniformity which was bitterly opposed in the south where nonconformity stretched as far back as the Visigoths who had embraced Arianism.

The revolution which swept away the Bourbons at the end of the eighteenth century was triggered by the summoning in May 1789 of the States-General, which had not met since 1614, to remedy the country's desperate financial situation caused mainly by the wasteful wars of Louis XIV and the extravagance of the royal court at Versailles. The crippling taxes were levied almost exclusively on the Third Estate or commoners, so when a series of accidental events gave them the chance their representatives broke away from the States-General and set up the National Assembly which in one sweep abolished all the feudal rights and privileges and issued as a preamble to a new constitution the famous Declaration of the Rights of Man, inspired by the social writings of Rousseau and the eighteenth-century philosophers.

It is impossible here to consider the course of the revolution in any detail, so we shall simply pick out its highlights. On 21 September 1792 the National Convention proclaimed the French Republic—and a plaque on the wall of the Tuileries gardens in Paris marks the spot; Louis XVI was guillotined on 21 January 1793 in what is now the Place de la Concorde and the Reign of Terror began under the direction of Robespierre.

Robespierre's fall was succeeded in 1795 by the unwieldy Directory system of government with power shared between an upper and lower house and five directors, but one-man rule was soon restored in the person of the brilliant Corsican general, Napoleon Bonaparte, whose intrigues and successful military campaigns made him successively First Consul, sole Consul and finally, in 1804, Emperor.

Napoleon's legal and administrative reforms we shall see more of in the next chapter; here the dates of his downfall must suffice. The retreat from Moscow in 1812 with the wreck of the once magnificent *grande armée* marked the beginning of the end of France's most glorious epoch, symbolised by the Arc de Triomphe at the top of the Champs Elysées. Two years later he was in exile on Elba and the short-lived Hundred Days episode, when he rallied his veterans for a last win-or-lose-all battle, finished on the plain of Waterloo on 18 June 1815.

After the exciting upheaval of the revolution and the Empire, France sought calmer times with the restoration of the Bourbons in the person of Louis XVIII, but his successor Charles X, having forgotten nothing and learned nothing, was deposed in the revolution of the 'three glorious days' in July 1830, commemorated by the bronze column in the Place de la Bastille. The throne was offered to Charles's cousin Louis-Philippe, the liberal-minded Duke of Orleans who had fought in the revolutionary army.

Being acceptable neither to the royalists nor to the republicans, Louis-Philippe, who had taken the title of 'King of the French,' relied too much on unpopular ministers who antagonised the working classes pressing for socialist reforms. In 1848 a bloodless revolution, inspired by the socialists, easily overthrew the weakened monarchy and the Second Republic was proclaimed.

In France's first presidential election by universal male suffrage Louis Napoleon, nephew of the great Emperor, was elected President for four years, but following a *coup d'état* in December 1851 he proclaimed the Second Empire and a plebiscite a year later ratified him as Emperor with the title of Napoleon III. Once again France preferred one-man rule.

The Second Empire lasted only eighteen years, during which heavy industry expanded, railways were built and Baron Haussmann transformed Paris with splendid boulevards. But in foreign policy the régime made some foolish errors and played into the hands of the Prussian Chancellor Bismarck who tricked Napoleon into declaring war on 19 July 1870. The French army, ill-prepared, was surrounded at Sedan and forced to surrender and the Empire was overthrown.

The Third Republic was proclaimed and the war against the Prussians continued, but it was a hopeless struggle and under the terms of the peace treaty France lost Alsace and part of Lorraine. This humiliation left a bitter wound in every Frenchman which was only healed with the recovery of the lost provinces in 1918.

The Third Republic, which was voted by a majority of one in 1875 after the uprising of the Paris workers known as the Commune had been savagely repressed, proved to be the longest-lived of the four republics which France experienced between 1792 and 1958. Originally intended by the monarchists as a necessary interlude before the restoration of a king, the makeshift republic gradually came to be the protector of the vested interests of the urban middle classes and the peasant proprietors and a bulwark against the ambitions of the royalists and the extreme left.

A severe test for the young republic was the Dreyfus affair which deeply divided the country between 1894 and 1906. When doubts were raised about the guilt of Captain Alfred Dreyfus, a Jewish army officer who had been court-martialled and sentenced to life imprisonment for espionage, opinion was sharply divided between right-wing Catholic, army and anti-semitic elements on the one hand, who were opposed to a re-trial, and on the other hand republicans and anti-clericals who believed Dreyfus was the victim of a conspiracy. Dreyfus was finally cleared, but the passions aroused led to a series of anti-clerical laws which enforced the expulsion of many religious orders from France (1901) and the separation of Church and State (1905).

These measures were of course deeply resented by Catholics, especially the withdrawal of state-aid for Church schools which is still an issue in French politics. The Third Republic, with the anti-clerical Radical party firmly in control, quickly became identified with the notion of *laïcité* or secularisation, but after the declaration of war in 1914 the whole nation forgot its divisions and rallied to the *union sacrée*.

The *Entente Cordiale* in 1904 had brought France and Britain closer together than at any other time in their history in spite of imperial ambitions which conflicted occasionally as in the case of the Sudan and Morocco. The differences were settled, how-ever, and by 1914 the French Empire had expanded enormously. In 1875 it consisted of Algeria, parts of West Africa, the four pre-revolutionary colonies of Guiana, Martinique, Guadeloupe and Reunion, scattered settlements in the Pacific, five small enclaves in India, the colony of Cochin-China and the islands of St Pierre and Miquelon near Newfoundland.

By 1914 these overseas possessions were increased by the Protectorates of Tunisia, Morocco, Annam and Tonkin (these last two form with Cochin-China the Vietnam, Cambodia and Laos of today), the colony of Madagascar and the vast federa-tions of French West and Equatorial Africa.

The French losses in the First World War were appalling. About a million and a half Frenchmen were killed and the north and north-east, which had been the battlefield for four years, were utterly devastated. The recovery of the three *départements* of Alsace and Lorraine claimed by Bismarck in 1870 was a great boost to the national pride, but the weak governments of the inter-war years increased the disillusion with which the country watched the revival of Germany and prepared the way for the collapse in 1940.

In 1936 the country had reacted to the increasing threats of fascism by electing a Popular Front government of Radicals, Socialists and Communists under Léon Blum. In its two years in office the coalition initiated many social reforms but appeals by military experts like Colonel Charles de Gaulle for the modernisation of the army's equipment were ignored.

This unpreparedness and misguided reliance on the protection of the Maginot Line fortresses, which the German army easily outflanked, were paid for in the summer of 1940. Within a few weeks the French army surrendered, an armistice with Germany was signed permitting the occupation of two thirds of the country, and the parliament voted full powers to Marshal Pétain at Vichy which became the capital of the unoccupied part. The Third Republic, which had had an unexpectedly long life, was finally dead.

The history of the war years is too well known to be recounted here. From London General de Gaulle rallied the various elements which were prepared to resist the Germans, either openly as in the Free French forces or clandestinely from within France in the Resistance networks. The liberation of France by the Allies in 1944 ended this dark period in French history and the survivors were determined to build a new France from the ruins of the occupation and the Vichy régime.

The constitution of the Fourth Republic was accepted in October 1946 after prolonged wrangling between the traditional parties and the Communists who had emerged the strongest after the liberation. General de Gaulle had resigned as provisional leader of the government the previous January when he saw that his proposals for a system with a strong executive protected from excessive parliamentary interference was not acceptable to the parties.

The Fourth Republic, in spite of governmental instability, got the crippled country on its feet again with the help of American aid and a series of national plans. Through far-sighted projects like the Schuman Plan for the co-ordination of Europe's coal and steel industries (1950) and the European Economic Community (1957), successive French governments played leading roles in the search for European unity, but the decolonisation problem, first in Indo-China (1954) and later in North Africa, proved too difficult for a régime which had lost the confidence of the nation.

In May 1958 General de Gaulle was called back from his retirement in the village of Colombey-les-deux-Eglises following a *coup d'état* by Algerian settlers backed by the army in Algeria. He became head of the government on 1 June and the Constitution of the Fifth Republic was accepted by referendum on 28 September. The General was elected President of the Republic on 21 December with a majority of 78.5 per cent of the votes of the electoral college. He was re-elected to a second seven-year term on 19 December 1965 under the new system of universal suffrage but resigned dramatically on 28 April 1969 following the adverse vote in a referendum on regional reform and the transformation of the Senate. His successor Georges Pompidou was elected the following June.

THE POPULATION

When the census taken in March 1968 revealed that the total population of France was slightly under 50 million, there was some official embarrassment as, about six months previously, the attainment of the 50 million mark had been celebrated with much ceremony. The experts explained that they had miscalculated the number of immigrants but that it was beyond doubt that the population had reached 50 million by September 1968. The population of Great Britain excluding Northern Ireland was about $53\frac{1}{2}$ million at the 1966 census.

Britain is thus much more densely populated than France, which is more than twice her size. The comparative densities are for England and Wales 791 persons to the square mile and for France only 210 persons to the square mile. If Scotland is taken into account the former figure falls to approximately 560. The United States of America is almost twenty times larger in area than France and with a population of just over 200 million is four times less densely populated than France.

It is worth while comparing briefly the population trends in the three countries since 1800. In 1801 the population of England and Wales was 8.8 million and that of France 27.3 million. One hundred years later the figures were 32.5 million and 38.9 million. In other words the population of England and Wales had practically quadrupled while that of France had increased by only forty-two per cent. This phenomenal increase in Britain is attributed to the Industrial Revolution and the resultant exodus of the rural population to the towns, whereas in France rapid industrialisation was hindered by the limited and scattered nature of the coal and iron ore resources. The population growth in the United States of America over the same period was even more spectacular, bounding from five million to ninety million, but of course massive immigration must be taken into account.

Other factors which may have discouraged a high birth rate in France in the nineteenth century were the Napoleonic inheritance law, which required that estates be divided up equally among all the children, and the climate of political instability provoked by the succession of régimes.

From 1900 to the outbreak of World War II the French population actually decreased as deaths continued to outnumber births and the terrible losses in men of World War I took their effect in a reduced marriage rate. Even the anti-birth-control law passed in 1920 outlawing contraceptives failed to check the falling birth rate. The immigration of about three million foreign workers, mainly Italians and Poles, filled out the total for the 1931 census to 41.8 million.

After the war a totally unexpected resurgence changed this depressing situation dramatically. Between 1946 and 1962 the population jumped from 40.5 million to 46.5 million, but the estimated three million increase in the past five years alone has been even more spectacular. Demographic experts have been baffled by this upsurge. In 1959 they estimated that the fifty million mark would be reached in 1990. They were hopelessly wrong by twenty-three years!

They had failed to take into account the importance of the rise in the birth rate coupled with the increased life expectancy, but an unforeseeable factor was the massive repatriation of officials and settlers from the overseas territories which gained their independence. Between 1954 and 1962 more than a million persons were repatriated, the climax being reached in 1962, the year of Algerian independence, when the influx totalled 650,000.

But what expert could have dared predict in 1946 that the French population would increase by nine million in twenty years whereas in the previous eighty-five years it had increased a mere 2.7 millions? It is no wonder that today France is experiencing such a shortage of housing, schools, hospitals and motorways.

Why did the French start reproducing at such a rate in 1946 (twenty-one births per 1,000 inhabitants)? It is generally accepted that the explanation for the phenomenon was the introduction of generous children's allowances and family benefits under the *Code de la Famille* drawn up in 1939 but not fully enforced until after the war. Sociologists also put forward the theory that the experience of two world wars destroyed the traditional appeal for the French of a static society best preserved by limiting families to one or two children.

The high birth rate of the immediate post-war years has been gradually diminishing and from 18.2 per thousand inhabitants in 1963 had descended to 17.4 in 1966 compared to 18.5 in U.S.A. In 1967 the anti-birth-control law was revoked and the sale of contraceptives was legalised on a doctor's prescription. This factor was expected to have an adverse effect on the birth rate in the the coming years. The infant mortality rate is less of a black spot in France than it used to be. From 25.6 per thousand in 1963 the national average has fallen to 21 in 1966, but this still compares unfavourably to other European countries such as Holland (14.8). The reason usually given is the lack of medical facilities in the isolated country districts, but it has been pointed out that the figure for highly industrialised areas in the north (36.1) is higher than in the deserted regions of the Central Plateau.

The general mortality rate had reached its lowest point in 1966 with 10.6 deaths per 1,000 inhabitants, but there is disquiet at the difference in life expectancy between men (sixty-eight) and women (seventy-five). The principal reason for the disparity may be, it is thought, the higher incidence of alcoholism among men, especially in rural areas.

The flight from the land which was such a noteworthy feature in nineteenth-century Britain only began to operate on a large scale in France after the war. Between 1954 and 1962 the active farming population fell by twenty-five per cent as 150,000 people left the countryside annually for the towns. Thus by 1962 the rural population was only thirty-eight per cent of the total compared to seventy-six per cent in 1846. In U.S.A. the rural population is reckoned at six per cent of the total.

The most heavily depopulated areas in France are the mountainous regions of the Alps, Pyrenees, Central Plateau, Vosges and Jura, the east and north-east of the Paris basin and the western half of the country generally.

The substantial increase of 3.6 million inhabitants between 1954 and 1962 was very unevenly distributed, as about eighty per cent of the increase was concentrated in the Paris region, Alsace, Lorraine, the Nord department and the regions of Rhône-Alpes and Provence-Côte d'Azur. Paris alone absorbed one-third of the increase.

In spite of the rural exodus to the urban areas, French towns and cities are small by British and American standards. At the 1968 census only Paris, Marseilles, Lyons, Lille and Bordeaux exceeded the half million mark. Apart from Paris, forty-nine towns in France have more than 100,000 people and thirteen of these exceed the 300,000 mark.

Paris and the surrounding *départements* or counties now number 9.1 million people and grew by almost two million between 1954 and 1962, although the population of the central area known as the *Ville de Paris* actually fell by almost 100,000 to 2.7 million. Cities in the provinces have also revealed the same movement from the centre to the suburbs. The fastest-growing towns are Grenoble, Caen and Besançon, where the populations increased between thirty-five and forty-five per cent.

The astonishing growth of the population of France since the war conceals some curious factors. Thus the active population remained almost stable in these years and the impressive post-war reconstruction programme was only possible with the aid of immigrant labour and substantial overtime. About one-third of the population is under twenty years of age and twelve per cent is over sixty-five, which means that for every hundred persons working there are ninety unemployed and a charge on the community as a whole.

RELIGION

Nine-tenths of the population are baptised Roman Catholics, but only one adult in five is estimated to fulfil the obligation of attending Mass on Sundays. The rest are nominal Catholics whose contact after childhood with the Church will probably be limited to the marriage service, the baptism of their children and the burial service. The most Catholic parts of France are Brittany in the west, Alsace in the east, and the south of the Central Plateau. Relatively more practising Catholics are found among women and the wealthier sections of the population than among the working class.

Protestants in France number about 800,000 and are divided among the six churches which make up the *Fédération Protestante de France*. The three Reformed Churches have 500,000 members and the remainder belong to the two Lutheran Churches and the Baptist Church. In recent years the churches have drawn closer together within the Federation and there is a strong movement in favour of forming one evangelical church. The Bas-Rhin department in Alsace has the highest proportion of Protestants (twenty-eight per cent) followed by the Gard in the south (seventeen per cent); Paris numbers about 60,000 and they are found mainly among the professions and the upper grades of the civil service, although thirty per cent of the total are farmers and workers.

The Jewish community, said to be one of the most active in

western Europe, numbers about 500,000 divided mainly among Paris, Marseilles and Alsace, although small groups are scattered all over France. During the war 115,000 Jews were deported to concentration camps and few returned.

To conclude this section on the population it is interesting to note the similarities in the vital statistics between France and England and Wales as the following table shows.

1964	Marriages	Divorces	Living births	Deaths
France	347,700	29,500	875,500	517,200
England and Wales	359,307	34,868	875,972	534,737
U.S.A.	1,720,000	445,000	4,027,490	1,798,051

THE LANGUAGE

French is a romance language derived from the Latin spoken by the legionaries during the Roman occupation. The old Celtic tongue used by the Gauls gradually died out except in the extreme west, but some words passed into the half Latin, half teutonic dialects emerging in the northern half of the country.

A definite division became established between the northern and southern dialects, which became known respectively as the

———

People. A typical café scene in Paris. The two waiters, called *garçons*, literally 'boys,' are wearing the traditional black suits. For those who want to pass several hours on the terrace there is plenty of reading matter on the newspaper kiosk behind. The kiosks usually replace the newsboys so familiar in Britain and the United States.

Brittany is one of the most Catholic parts of France. The two women entering the church are wearing the traditional costume of the Vannes region in south Brittany. Each region of the old province has its distinctive lace head-dress.

Langue d'Oil and the *Langue d'Oc*, from the words for ' yes.'
The latter dialect remained closer to the Latin as the south was
more influenced by Roman culture. This division was further
emphasised in the twelfth and thirteenth centuries when Roman
law was revived in the south and, as the *droit écrit*, was in force
until the revolution.

In the north the dialect called *Francien* spoken by the Franks
in the Paris region came to dominate the others and its influence
spread as the Capetian kings extended their sway and the court
and university became the centre of artistic, literary and scientific
movements. In the sixteenth century the use of French was made
compulsory throughout the kingdom, ousting Latin as the
language of royal edicts. The Norman conquest of England
resulted, of course, in the widespread use of French as the
language of the court, the ruling classes and of legal documents.
By Chaucer's time in the fourteenth century English itself was
heavily infiltrated by French words and has remained so.

In 1635 the French Academy was founded by Richelieu, and
its forty members, called *Immortels*, were charged with writing
the official dictionary which would ensure the *bon usage* of the
language. The work of the Academy is still going on and in
1967 the *Immortels* had reached the letter C in the ninth revision

———

A Parisian couple chat in the sun on the Ile Saint-Louis behind
Notre Dame cathedral. The French tend to marry young,
the men at twenty-three after military service, the women at
twenty or twenty-one. In three out of four marriages husband
and wife are from the same region and belong to the same
social milieu. Between the two world wars the average family
had two children, but now three is regarded as the ideal by
most families. The sale and publicity of artificial birth control
methods was illegal until 1967. For every ten marriages in
France each year there is an average of one divorce.

of the dictionary which began in 1935 and at the present rate will finish in 2125.

The prestige of the court of Louis XIV at Versailles and the brilliance of French poets, playwrights and philosophers spread the knowledge of French throughout Europe in the seventeenth and eighteenth centuries. It remained the language of diplomacy until the Treaty of Versailles in 1919.

Today it is estimated that French is spoken by 150 million people, being the official language in twenty-four countries and the medium of education in seven others. It is in the former colonies, of course, that the French language and culture achieved its greatest influence overseas, but today 1,000 branches of the *Alliance Française* all over the world teach French to about 120,000 students.

Several other languages or dialects (*patois*) are still spoken in border areas of France. In Alsace a German dialect is quite common and in the north Flemish can be heard around Dunkirk. In the west the old Celtic tongue, Breton, is used by the older people and by those who are in favour of more autonomy for the region. It is not uncommon for Breton parents to fight for years in the courts for the right to call their children by Breton names which do not figure in the approved calendar. At the western end of the Pyrenees, Basque is still spoken and at the eastern end of the range in Roussillon a little Catalan. In Provence the old *patois* known as Provençal has retained a hold and was used by the poet Mistral. Finally in Corsica the natives speak an Italian dialect as well as French.

NATIONAL CHARACTERISTICS

The French people display many of the characteristics associated with the Latin temperament. They are demonstrative, voluble, animated and frequently gay, enlivening conversations with gestures and mimicry. In dress the men tend to be conservative, even dowdy, while with women there is a sharp division corresponding to social categories. The superb taste shown by those who can afford the *haute couture* styles is not as widespread as foreigners imagine, possibly because French ready-to-wear clothes can be poor in quality in spite of prices high by American and British standards.

But these are superficial traits quickly apparent to even the unobservant. What lies behind the gallic exterior, the eyebrow-raising, the shoulder-shrugging and the grimaces which General de Gaulle, for example, practised with such artistry during his press conferences?

Foreign observers, it must be admitted, are often critical about the French character. Matthew Arnold wrote that ' France was fam'd in all great arts, in none supreme,' and Dr Johnson complained that ' a Frenchman must always be talking whether he knows anything of the matter or not.' But the French, as we have seen, are derived from such a hoch-potch of European races that generalisations are not very reliable.

The dour Flemish miner in the Nord, a beer drinker and a soccer fan, would seem to have more in common with an English north countryman than with a fiery vineyard owner in the Midi, fond of drinking the local aniseed-flavoured Pastis and spending hours playing *boules* under the Mediterranean sun.

One trait the French themselves would probably agree they have in common is an innate *méfiance* or distrust of human nature which is commonly described as cynicism. But fortunately the Frenchman's cynicism does not prevent him from being one of the most tolerant persons in the world. The Declaration of the Rights of Man has found concrete expression in the thousands of political refugees and exiles who have found a second home in France. Racism, while not unknown in France, is clearly repugnant to the vast majority and nothing unusual was seen in the fact that the deputy head of state, M Gaston Monnerville, who had been President of the Senate for many years, is a Negro.

It should be added, however, that for the French tolerance remains on a philosophical level and in everyday life their emotional temperament often leads them to be quick-tempered and sharp-tongued. But such outbursts are quickly forgotten as a rule. Behind the steering-wheel tempers can flare following the most minor incidents, and after a series of violent sequels to differences between drivers a national newspaper distributed thousands of windscreen stickers with the appeal ' Let's keep our tempers '. They seemed to work—for a time.

Perhaps the last word on the French character should be left to the person who summed it up as follows :

This Frenchman, who takes so much pain to be orderly in his thinking and so little in his actions, this logician always torn by doubt, this careless hard worker, this imperial adventurer who loves nothing more than his hearth at home, this fervent admirer of alexandrine verses, tailcoats and royal gardens, who none the less sings popular songs, dresses carelessly and litters his own lawns . . . this uncertain, unstable and contradictory people.

These words were written by General de Gaulle forty years ago.

2

How the Country is Run

THE CONSTITUTION

ON 16 May 1946, four months after he had resigned as premier of the provisional post-war government, General de Gaulle made a speech at Bayeux in Normandy in which he outlined his ideal constitution. The French temperament, he observed, did not submit easily to government, and strong institutions were needed 'to compensate for the effects of our perpetual effervescence.' These institutions consisted essentially of a powerful executive derived from the president who would have the right to name the prime minister and other ministers, preside at cabinet meetings, promulgate laws, issue decrees and call elections.

The following October the Constitution of the Fourth Republic was narrowly accepted by a referendum in which there were over eight million abstentions. Full powers were vested in the National Assembly and, as no party obtained an absolute majority in the general election the following month, the Assembly was able to overthrow coalition governments at will and the president's role was virtually limited to designating the successive prime ministers who might or might not receive investiture.

As General de Gaulle foretold, no government could survive long under such a system and there were no fewer than nineteen between December 1946 and May 1958 as well as numerous reshuffles. When after twelve years in the political wilderness the general returned to power on 1 June 1958 following the army *coup d'état* in Algeria, he appointed a small ministerial committee to draft a new Constitution which was submitted to and amended by a consultative committee mainly composed of Members of Parliament. On 28 September 1958 almost eighty per cent of the population, including those in the overseas territories, voted in favour of the new Constitution and the Fifth Republic came into being a week later.

It was no surprise to find the principles laid down at Bayeux enshrined in the new Constitution. The presidency has now become considerably more important. As head of state, the President is also head of the armed forces. He appoints the Prime Minister and the other ministers proposed by the latter. He promulgates the laws voted by Parliament and can send them back for reconsideration but not veto them. He appoints to all the high civil and military offices and presides over the Council of Ministers and the High Councils of Defence. He can send messages to the National Assembly, ratifies treaties negotiated in his name and has the power of pardon. He lives in the eighteenth century Elysée Palace, near the British Embassy in the Rue Faubourg St-Honoré.

Most of these functions approximate to those performed by presidents under previous régimes, but the new Constitution conferred three additional powers on the President which considerably increased his scope of action. First, he can dissolve the National Assembly and call a general election, but a year must elapse before he can do so again. Secondly he can submit certain Bills to the electorate in a referendum on the proposal of the Government or Parliament. Thirdly Article 16 allows him to assume emergency powers 'when the institutions of the Republic, the independence of the Nation, the integrity of its territory or the fulfilment of its international commitments are threatened with immediate and grave danger.' General de Gaulle used these powers during several months in 1961 following the generals' revolt in Algeria.

No French president had ever been accorded such extensive powers, but when General de Gaulle was elected head of state on 21 December 1958 he proceeded to interpret several of them in a way which increased their range even further. This was especially so in the case of Article 11, which says that the President may submit to referendum a government Bill dealing with the organisation of the public authorities, the French Community and treaties, but only on the proposal of Parliament or the Government. In practice the General used referendums on his own initiative for several questions in the settlement of the Algerian war. In November 1962 he asked the country to approve a change in the method of electing the President, substituting universal suffrage for the restricted electoral college. This action was severely criticised as not in accordance with the Constitution but the General continued to interpret it in ways which have modified its character.

The Government, according to Article 20, ' decides and directs the policy of the nation ' and is responsible to Parliament. The Prime Minister is responsible for national defence and ministers are not allowed to be Members of Parliament. If they stand for election and win a seat they must resign and a substitute (*suppléant*) who is named before the election replaces them. If a Member of Parliament dies the same procedure is followed; a by-election takes place if a Member resigns.

Parliament is composed of the National Assembly and the Senate, but for the first time the matters on which Parliament may legislate are enumerated and all others must be left to the Government. Parliament may for a temporary period authorise the Government to issue ordinances on matters which are normally within the province of law. In June 1967 the Government, against strong opposition, obtained from Parliament powers to rule by decree in economic affairs for almost six months.

The regularity of presidential elections and referendums is ensured by the Constitutional Council, which must also be consulted on the conformity with the Constitution of certain laws and by the President if he intends to assume emergency powers. The High Court of Justice can try presidents on charges of high treason and ministers and their accomplices accused of plotting against the security of the state. Arraignment depends on both Houses passing identical motions by an absolute majority of their members.

The first article of the Constitution states that 'the Republic and those peoples of the overseas territories who, by an act of free determination, adopt the present constitution set up a Community.' In a later section twelve articles deal with the administrative machinery of the Community, but by the time this had been set up the Community had virtually ceased to exist as conceived by the Constitution and amendments were passed in June 1960 to take account of the changed circumstances.

The situation today is as follows. The French Republic consists of the ninety-five metropolitan departments; the four overseas departments of Martinique, Guadeloupe, Reunion and Guiana, which are completely assimilated with France but enjoy a measure of autonomy in local administration; the seven overseas territories of French Polynesia, New Caledonia, French Somaliland, Comoro Archipelago, Saint-Pierre and Miquelon, Southern and Antarctic territories and Wallis and Futuna Islands, all poor and sparsely-inhabited and controlled by various statutes. The Community consists formally of the French Republic and the Republics of Central Africa, the Congo (Brazzaville), Gabon, Malagasy, Senegal and Chad. Finally, special relations have been established between France and the following Republics—Ivory Coast, Dahomey, Upper Volta, Mauritania, Niger, Cameroun, Mali and Togo.

In practice the Community as an institution is a dead letter and the six African members have full sovereignty and are members of the United Nations. They all continue to benefit considerably from French financial aid and technical and cultural co-operation, as do France's other former possessions.

PARLIAMENT

Parliament, as we have seen, consists of the National Assembly and the Senate, the French bicameral system more or less corresponding to the House of Commons and the House of Lords in Britain, as the Senate has only the power to delay legislation and not block it unless the Government allows this. The National Assembly sits in the Palais-Bourbon overlooking the Seine opposite the Place de la Concorde; the Senate in the seventeenth century Luxembourg Palace, also on the Left Bank.

Parliament normally meets for two sessions during the year. The first session begins in October and lasts eighty days; it is mostly devoted to the debates and vote on the budget for the following year. The second session begins in April and may not last more than ninety days. Extraordinary sessions may be called at the request of the Prime Minister or a majority of the members of the Assembly.

A member cannot be prosecuted for any opinions expressed or votes cast by him in the exercise of his functions. Members are no longer allowed to vote by proxy except for special reasons such as illness and the British pairing system is not used. This ruling is an attempt to eliminate the widespread absenteeism which characterised the Fourth Republic and as a further encouragement there is an attendance bonus. It is doubtful if these measures have had the hoped-for success and on various occasions ministers have complained that lack of questions has prevented them from making speeches on important subjects. Members are paid the same salaries as the highest-grade civil servants, which in 1967 amounted to 6,500 francs a month ($16,000 a year, £5,600). Article 27 of the Constitution declares that mandatory instructions to a member from outside parliament are null and void, but this does not prevent members voting according to party policy. The object of the rule seems to be to protect members from pressure groups, but so far there has not been a satisfactory interpretation.

The running of both Houses is carried on by the *bureau,* consisting of the President, who corresponds to the Speaker in the House of Representatives, assisted by a number of vice-presidents and secretaries. There are six permanent Parliamentary Commissions for cultural and social affairs, foreign affairs, defence, finance, constitutional laws and production and commerce. Only

groups consisting of thirty or more parliamentarians are represented on commissions. Temporary *ad hoc* commissions can
also be set up for special subjects such as the reform of the anti-
birth control laws.

Bills can be introduced in either House except finance Bills
which must have their first reading in the Assembly. Private
members' Bills are not in order if they entail a decrease in
revenue or an increase in expenditure. After a Bill is introduced
it is submitted to the appropriate commission which reports on
it and may propose amendments. In the case of a government
Bill, the minister responsible pilots it through the House which
debates it article by article after hearing the minister's declaration
and the commission's report. A Fifth Republic innovation much
resented by the opposition is the minister's power to refuse to
consider any amendment not previously submitted to the commission and to insist on a single vote (*vote bloqué*) for all or part
of the Bill including only those amendments proposed or approved by the Government. After the first reading and vote in the
Assembly the Bill goes to the Senate for a similar procedure. In
the case of disagreement the bill shuttles back and forth between
the two Houses but the Government is able to override the
Senate if it wishes.

The Assembly's control over the Government under the Fifth
Republic is subject to rigid rules. For the first time the Assembly's
powers of legislation are expressly delimited and snap defeats of
governments are no longer possible. The Government can only
be forced to resign if it is defeated (1) when the Prime Minister
has pledged its responsibility, (2) in a vote of censure which
cannot take place less than forty-eight hours after it has been
tabled and must be voted by a majority of the effective membership of the Assembly, and (3) if the Prime Minister makes an
issue a matter of confidence and a vote of censure is tabled and
carried.

The aim of these rules was to eliminate as far as possible the
instability which characterised the governments of the Fourth
Republic. In a sense the rules have proved their worth, as since
1958 the Government has only been forced to resign once, in

October 1962, and the succeeding legislature was the first one since the war to run its full course and not be marked by the fall of a government. But this was possible, not because of the rules, but because the Gaullist party, the Union for the New Republic (UNR), and its ally the Independent Republicans had 269 seats in the 482-seat Assembly and the defeat of the Government was never a possibility.

The political scene in France for the whole of the first decade of the Fifth Republic was completely dominated by General de Gaulle and his ' personal rule ' style of government. M Debré, M Pompidou and M Couve de Murville as successive prime ministers were completely overshadowed by the personality of the General, who ruled the country less as an ' arbiter,' which was the role the Constitution assigned to him, than as a chief executive enforcing his personal policies by means of referendums, direct appeals to the people on radio and television and then merely communicating his decisions to the Council of Ministers. In a witty understatement the General observed at one of his press conferences ' We have not become President to inaugurate chrysanthemums,' referring to the more formal figurehead role traditionally associated with presidents of the Republic.

The sudden resignation of the General in April 1969 shocked France and indeed most of the world but the ' chaos ' which Gaullists had so often prophesied would overwhelm the country without the stabilising presence of the stern father-figure did not materialise, and the election of the former Prime Minister, M Georges Pompidou, proceeded in an orderly and calm fashion. The immediate cause of the General's resignation was the rejection in a referendum of his complicated proposals to downgrade the Senate, dominated by political opponents, and to introduce greater autonomy for the regions.

There still remains the mystery as to why the General tied his political future to the outcome of the referendum, an action which commentators described as ' political suicide,' as it became apparent that the country felt little enthusiasm for the proposed reforms especially that dealing with the Senate. At the height of the rioting the previous year the General had promised a referendum on unspecified reforms which had to be postponed, and a general election took place instead which confirmed the strength of the Gaullists. The orderly transmission of power from General de Gaulle to his successor was a testimony to the basic democratic sense of the French people and to the soundness of the institutions of the Fifth Republic.

The 1967 election had cut the Gaullist majority to a handful but the June 1968 election, called after the student and labour upheavals, altered the situation dramatically. For the first time the Gaullists had an absolute majority in the National Assembly and no longer needed the sometimes grudging support of the Independent Republicans, a conservative group led by M Valéry Giscard d'Estaing. The left-wing federation, grouping Socialists and Radicals, and the Communists, lost over half their seats in the Gaullist landslide although their share of the popular vote was surprisingly well maintained.

The National Assembly parliamentary groups were divided as follows after the 1968 election:

MAJORITY		OPPOSITION	
Union of Democrats for		Progress and Modern	
the Republic (Gaullists)	292	Democracy	33
Independent Republicans	62	Left-wing Democratic and	
	——	Socialist Federation	57
	354	Communists	34
	——	Others	9
			——
			133
			——

ELECTORAL SYSTEM

Since the Revolution various régimes have experimented with almost every conceivable electoral system with the general aim of assuring the representation of the multiple factions which composed the electorate. Under the Fifth Republic there has been a noticeable trend towards simplification in the hope that gradually the multi-party system will be resolved into a few, if possible two or three, big groups. At present elections to the National Assembly, which take place every five years unless there is a dissolution, are by means of the single member system with two ballots. A candidate is successful by obtaining an absolute majority of the votes cast in the first ballot or, if he fails to do this, by heading the poll at the second ballot a week later. Candidates who fail to obtain ten per cent of the votes of all those inscribed on the electoral register in the first round are eliminated and lose their deposits as well as the right to be reimbursed by the state for the cost of the prescribed electoral posters. All citizens over the age of twenty-one not deprived of their civic rights are entitled to vote.

The system for the Senate is more complicated. Candidates are elected by a college in each department consisting of the parliamentary deputies, the departmental councillors and a representation of the municipal councillors from all the communes. The method of voting varies according to the size of the departments. Senators are elected for nine years, a third retiring every three years. The minimum age is thirty-five. They tend to be *notables* in their own localities such as mayors, big landowners, lawyers or doctors.

Presidential elections since the referendum of November 1962 are by universal suffrage. The system is similar to that for the Assembly : elections with two ballots, an absolute majority being required for victory in the first one and a simple majority in the second. A sensation was caused when General de Gaulle failed to win an outright victory in the first round of the presidential election in 1965.

POLITICAL PARTIES

Remarkable progress has been made under the Fifth Republic towards a simplification of the French political scene with its once amazing multiplicity of parties, most of them small and insignificant. A recent study shows that during the Third

Republic there were fifty-two political parties, although many of these were not represented in Parliament. In contrast, for the second ballot of the March 1967 election the contest for control of the National Assembly was fought out between four groups, the Fifth Republic group (a title created for the election and consisting of the Gaullist UNR party, its Independent Republican allies and a dozen or so moderates), the Left Wing Democratic and Socialist Federation (grouping the Socialists, Radicals and left-wing political clubs known as the Convention), the Communist party and the Centre Democratic party. There was a handful of candidates either unattached or from splinter parties like the Unified Socialist party of M Mendès-France.

This line-up represented a transformation of the traditional framework of French politics and was interpreted as an important step towards a two-party system as in Britain and the United States, with the Gaullists and their allies as a future conservative party and the Federation and the Communists, who had agreed on a highly successful electoral pact, as the foundation of a broad-based labour party provided their ideological differences could be settled.

The most interesting development in French politics in the 1960s was the attempt to build up the Federation into a cohesive left-wing force which could challenge the Gaullist dominance. The attempt made by M Mitterrand to merge the two oldest parties, the Radicals (1901) and the Socialists (1905) whose full title was Section Française de l'Internationale Ouvrière or SFIO, was continually frustrated by party rivalries; he gave up the effort at the end of 1968.

Early in 1969 the Socialists gave themselves a new title and the Radicals made a last effort to save themselves from total eclipse by appointing the dynamic publisher, M Servan-Schreiber, to a top post. But the democratic Left seems unable to escape from the uncomfortable fact that it can only come to power with the aid of the Communists.

The French Communist party was born from a split in the Socialist Party at the 1920 congress and it has remained almost embarrassingly faithful to Moscow ever since. Since the war it has won an average of five million votes in each election, except in 1958 when a million of its voters deserted to support General de Gaulle. With such powerful support in the country the Communists hold the key to any attempt by the left to gain power. The party, with an official membership of 430,000 mainly in the Paris region, the industrial north and the wine-growing Midi, had become more acceptable to the middle-classes and had hoped to work out a common programme with the Federation following its spectacular success in the 1967 election in winning seventy-three seats compared to forty-one in the previous election. The 1968 election was a disaster and since then the party has been most worried by the threat to its traditional support from the Maoists and other ultra-left groups.

The 1967 election had proved a severe fright for the Gaullists and their precarious majority barely survived a series of Opposition censure motions in the year that followed. The May 1968 crisis, sparked off by student rioting in the Latin Quarter of Paris, caught the regime, and indeed the whole country, completely unawares as the absence abroad at critical times of both General de Gaulle and the Premier, M Pompidou, testified.

The student rioting was, however, a less serious threat to the regime than the general strike which involved about ten million workers and virtually paralysed the country. Inspired by the student occupation of the Sorbonne and the Odéon Theatre in Paris, workers and even professional people all over the country, spontaneously occupied factories and administrative headquarters, claiming a greater say in the running of their affairs.

By the last week of May, even General de Gaulle seemed to have lost control of the situation and both students and left wing strikers began to call for a change of Government. The turning point came on 30 May when General de Gaulle broadcast to the nation following a tour of army headquarters where he received pledges of loyalty. The General galvanised his supporters and dismayed his opponents with a brief, fighting speech scotching rumours of his resignation and calling for a new parliamentary election. The election resulted in a runaway Gaullist victory and established the party more strongly than ever before. General de Gaulle then dismissed M Pompidou, hinting that he should prepare himself for the Presidency at some future date, and appointed in his place, M Maurice Couve de Murville, Minister of Foreign Affairs since 1958.

When M Pompidou became president in 1969, he appointed M Chaban-Delmas as Prime Minister. Others who returned to the Government were M Giscard d'Estaing and M Maurice Schumann, for Finance and Foreign Affairs respectively.

THE CIVIL SERVICE

The highly centralised nature of the system of administration in France, with its origins going back to pre-Revolutionary times, has meant that the Civil Service or *fonction publique* has a greater influence than in Britain and the United States. In 1950 the number of non-industrial civil servants in France was 1,095,000 or 2.6 per cent of the population compared to 684,000 or 1.4 per cent of the population in Britain for example.

The principal reason for the difference is that in France the number of civil servants is swelled by almost half a million teachers employed by the Ministry of Education. On the other hand about 1.5 million persons are employed in Britain by the

———

Parisians engaged in one of the most popular national pastimes within sight of the Ile de la Cité in the middle of the Seine, on which Paris was founded. The island is dominated by the twin towers of Notre Dame cathedral, finished in 1245, and the soaring spire of the Sainte-Chapelle, another Gothic masterpiece. The rest of the island is largely taken up by the Law Courts, the Prefecture of Police and the grim Conciergerie where most of the Revolution's most illustrious victims, including Marie-Antoinette, were imprisoned before execution.

A large proportion of French people still live in old, shabby buildings such as these in Montmartre in Paris. Often they are overcrowded with immigrant workers and lack proper toilet facilities.

local government services compared with 550,000 in France.

The French Civil Service has played an extremely important role by ensuring administrative continuity amid revolutions, *coups d'état* and the fall of governments, but one of the drawbacks which resulted from this predominance was the increasing independence and influence of the *grands corps*, such as Inspectors of Finance and Councillors of State. Recruiting for these high administrative posts was controlled by the *corps* and between the wars they became a privileged caste in the Civil Service.

Post-war reforms in 1946 and 1959, based partly on the British model, have attempted to make the administrative class more homogeneous by limiting the isolationism of the *grand corps* and making recruiting more democratic. Thus a civil service division or *Direction Generale* was set up to supervise the whole service under the control of the Prime Minister. Four general classes A, B, C and D, corresponding to administrative, executive, clerical and typist grades, were instituted, two non-specialised corps of administrators and executives were to gradually replace departmental specialists, and for training the *Ecole Nationale d'Administration* was set up.

Successful candidates in the stiff ENA entrance examination

———

Two vastly different 'Castles of the Loire.' The Château de Chenonceaux, built between 1513 and 1521, spans the Loire's tributary the Cher. Its most famous occupant was Catherine de Medici and among the distinguished figures who visited there was Mary Stuart, Queen of Scotland and France by her marriage to François II.

The Chinon nuclear power station of Electricité de France in the Loire valley has three reactors in service, able to produce 750 megawatts. The EDF is building three more gas-graphite nuclear power stations, using natural uranium, to be in service by 1971. They will have a combined capacity of over 2,000 megawatts. By the end of the seventies the EDF plans to be using fast breeder reactors and prototypes are being tested at the Cadarache research centre in the Rhône valley.

are drawn from both university graduates and the executive grade. The three-year training includes a period of practical experience, usually in the central government's external services in the provinces. The cream of these recruits still go into the *grands corps* and the rest become general administrators.

The technical administrative posts are filled from specialised training colleges such as the famous *Ecole Polytechnique* set up during the Revolution and adapted by Napoleon for the training of army engineers and civil servants. Other institutes which are really post-graduate schools train mining and road engineers, revenue officials, future prefects and educational administrators. Entrance to the executive and clerical grades is usually by direct examination by the different departments.

Conditions of employment for French civil servants are generally satisfactory in the administrative and executive grades, with a differential salary scale and generous allowances, but frequent strikes have expressed the discontent of the clerical and manual grades. The police are forbidden by law to strike, and since 1963 five days' notice must be given of any strike by central and local government employees and those in public enterprise responsible for a public service. Relations between the State and civil servants are chiefly handled by two joint committees and the National Civil Service Council.

LOCAL GOVERNMENT

In contrast to the Revolution's failure to endow France with a stable system of central government was its achievement in installing a system of local government which, completed by Napoleon, has survived a century and a half of wars and upheavals. Its framework is simple but rigid. In the place of the old provinces, each with their own customs, laws and privileges, the country was divided up into *départements*. Named after geographical features such as rivers and mountains, there are today ninety-five *départements* in metropolitan France. Each *département* is divided into *arrondissements* (313 in all), each *arrondissement* is divided into *cantons* (3,052 in all) and each *canton* into *communes* (37,962 in all).

In practice the department and the commune are the major units. At the head of the department is the prefect appointed by the central government. His powers and attributes are extremely wide, but basically the prefect is the representative of the State in the department, the head of all the government services, and has the task of keeping Paris informed of the political mood at any time but especially before elections. As the representative of the Minister of the Interior the prefect is the principal link in the chain of authority stretching from the central government to the mayors of the communes, and finally he is the chief executive of the local government system in the department.

Each department has a *conseil général*, like a county council, elected by universal suffrage for six years, half the councillors retiring every three years. The council has not much power. It meets for two sessions a year lasting not more than six weeks and votes the departmental budget prepared by the prefect. The budget expenses go mainly to roads, public assistance and transport. In 1961 they totalled 4.1 thousand million francs (approximately $820 million, £340 million). The main sources of revenue are rates and local sales taxes.

The communes are not artificial creations like the departments, but consist of all the towns, villages and sometimes parishes. Their enormous number is a serious handicap today when community services are becoming so complex. About 31,000 communes have less than 1,000 inhabitants and twenty per cent have less than 200.

The communes are run by municipal councils elected by universal suffrage every six years. The *maire*, elected by the council, is an extremely important figure and wears his tricolour sash of office on official occasions. Like the prefect, he is the representative of the State and as head of the police in small towns he is responsible for law and order, although he cannot appoint or replace members of the police force. His duties include the registration of births and deaths and conducting marriage ceremonies. Although elected by the municipal council, the mayor is independent in many matters and can only be suspended by the prefect if he fails to carry out his duties.

The municipal councils vary in size from nine members in villages to over sixty in Lyons and Marseilles. They meet four times a year and vote the budget. Most of the expenses go to the upkeep of the roads and the social services. In 1964 communal expenses totalled almost three billion dollars (£1,173 million). Government credits may be granted for improvement schemes and the poorer communes are financed from a common fund.

Because of the extension of the central government services into the provinces, especially in the cases of education and highways and bridges, there are far fewer full-time local government officials in France than in Britain. Excluding Paris there were 430,000 full-time local government officials in France in 1962 and 150,000 part-time, compared with about 1.5 million in Britain.

The most important source of local government revenue, the *taxe locale*, which is a two-and-three-quarter per cent tax on retail sales and an eight-and-a-half per cent tax on services, has been abolished and replaced by an added value tax.

Where communes wish to co-operate in the provision of services they are empowered to set up inter-communal syndicates. Where the communes are part of a conurbation these are called urban districts, but there has been a marked reluctance on the part of communes to give up even a part of their powers such as fire services and housing, and in 1964 there were only about forty urban districts. In 1966 the Government made it compulsory for several of the larger cities such as Lille and Lyons to create urban districts in the conurbations.

Because of its size Paris has always had a special system of local government. Another reason, of course, is that successive régimes have felt the need to keep a tight control over the capital with its reputation for hatching revolutions. Consequently there is no mayor of Paris but instead two prefects appointed by the Government. The Prefect of Police is responsible for law and order and the repression of crime and the Prefect of Paris for the administration of the twenty *arrondissements* of the city proper. In 1964 Parliament voted a reorganisation of the region which divided the department of the Seine into four new departments, one of which is Paris itself; the surrounding department of Seine-et-Oise was divided into three new departments.

Paris is thus unique in being both a city and a department. The prefect is assisted by a council of ninety members and the city remains divided into *arrondissements* like the London boroughs, each headed by a mayor appointed by the Government.

Even before this reform, the planning and development of what is known as the *district de Paris* or greater Paris area, where the population is expected to reach twelve millions within ten years, had been entrusted in 1961 to a new authority headed by a delegate-general, now called a prefect, responsible to the Prime Minister and administered by a council of twenty-eight members, half of whom are experts appointed by the Government and half of whom are elected members of the local authorities of the region. The authority's task is to plan and help to finance services for the region such as transport, hospitals and university faculties. One of the most important of these is the regional Metro express line which will link the outlying west and east suburbs to the central underground network. The authority has also drawn up a *schema* or master plan for the region in the year 2,000, which aims at counteracting the concentric ' oil stain ' type of expansion by concentrating future development along two axes about thirty miles north and south of the capital, parallel to the valley of the Seine.

On a national scale regional development is co-ordinated by a special agency raised in 1967 to a ministry attached to the Prime Minister. The department has long been recognised as too small a unit for efficient economic planning and in 1956 the country was divided into twenty-two regions, reduced in 1960 to twenty-one, which correspond ironically to the old provinces and indeed keep their names, for example, Brittany, Burgundy, Franche-Comté and Aquitaine. The prefect of the principal city in each region has become a ' super prefect ' with real powers over his colleagues for the distribution of government credits. He is advised by an Economic Development Committee of twenty to fifty members, consisting of departmental councillors, mayors, representatives of local chambers of commerce, industry and agriculture and experts appointed by the Government.

LEGAL SYSTEM

The most sweeping of the Revolutionary and Napoleonic reforms were in the legal and judicial systems, and the principles laid down then have largely survived up to the present, in spite of later modifications of which the most important was probably the reorganisation of the courts and criminal procedure introduced in December 1958.

The lowest courts are the 457 *tribunaux d'instance* (civil) and *tribunaux de police* (criminal) which deal with minor cases and offences. The police court can impose fines up to 2,000 francs ($400, £145) and sentences not exceeding two months. At the next level are the 172 *tribunaux de grande instance* (civil) and the *tribunaux correctionnels* (criminal) in which cases are heard by three judges but without a jury. The correctional courts hear the graver offences (*délits*) which are punishable with up to five years' imprisonment. Appeals from these courts are heard by the twenty-seven Appeal Courts. The more serious crimes such as murder are tried by the Courts of Assizes which sit in each department. The presiding judge is assisted by two magistrates and there is a jury of nine persons. Both judges and jury retire together to consider verdict and sentence. A two-thirds majority is necessary to reach a verdict. The death penalty for murder is still in force but very few persons have been guillotined in recent years.

There is no right of appeal from the Court of Assizes, but the highest court, called the Court of Cassation, can be asked to decide on a point of law or procedure in both criminal and civil matters. If the Court of Cassation quashes the judgment the case is sent for retrial by a different court.

A State Security Court, set up in 1963, consisting of military and civilian judges, tries charges of treason and subversion in peacetime. It has been occupied mainly with members of the illegal Secret Army Organisation (OAS) accused of plotting against the state by actively opposing the granting of independence to Algeria in 1962.

There are various specialised courts in civil matters, such as the *conseils de prud'hommes* which hear disputes between employers and employees with judges elected by both sides. Commercial disputes can be settled by the *tribunaux de commerce* composed of merchants elected for two years. Other special courts deal with social security matters and rent disputes. The advantage of these courts is that proceedings are simplified and cheap and save having recourse to more expensive litigation.

The way in which the French press often reports crimes and the arrest of suspected persons can give the impression that, contrary to the practice under British and U.S. law, in France an accused person is presumed guilty until found innocent. In fact this is not so, but in the case of serious offences there is a detailed preliminary investigation of the case by an examining magistrate (*juge d'instruction*). He interrogates the accused and confronts him with relevant witnesses and can also request the police to help him in his inquiry. The accused has the right to refuse to speak, however, except in the presence of his counsel. When the examining magistrate has finished his inquiry, if he decides there is a real case against the accused he sends the dossier to the Public Prosecutor. The magistrate also has the power to decide if the accused can be set free or not while awaiting trial. Preventive detention, as imprisonment before trial is called, is supposed to be exceptional but in practice it is widely used despite widespread criticism. In 1967 there were about 14,000 persons in jail awaiting trial, compared with about 5,000 in Britain. As French justice moves slowly—a two-year delay between arrest and trial is not uncommon in murder cases— persons who are subsequently found not guilty spend long periods in prison and may have to endure the additional humiliation of being condemned without a hearing by the less scrupulous sections of the press.

The procedure for criminal cases in court is quite unlike that in Britain and the United States. The judge plays a much more active role and conducts the case himself, questioning the accused and witnesses. Defence counsel can only put questions to witnesses through the judge, who may refuse them. Evidence which would not be admitted in a British court, such as intimate biographical details of the accused and even of witnesses, is allowed.

French judges are not appointed from the ranks of barristers, as in Britain, but enter the judiciary after a three-year training in a post-graduate school. They are civil servants but have a special status and cannot be given orders by the Government or dismissed except for breaches of discipline. The state prosecutors, who are also part of the judiciary, are less independent than the judges in the strict sense of the term and may be instructed by the Ministry of Justice on how to conduct a case.

The legal profession consists of five orders. The *avocats* correspond to barristers and they can appear in any court except the Court of Cassation. The functions of a solicitor are carried out by *avoués* and *notaires*, the former drafting legal documents for the use of *avocats* and the latter acting as legal adviser as well as drawing up contracts, wills and other documents. The *huissiers* and *greffiers* perform similar tasks to bailiffs and clerks of the court.

Mention should be made of the parallel system of administrative justice. Citizens can appeal to one of the twenty-four administrative courts throughout the country against what they regard as unjust decisions by the state. If the court finds that there was an irregularity it has power to redress it and order the aggrieved person to be compensated by the state. The Ombudsman in Sweden might be described as fulfilling a similar role, but the Parliamentary Commissioner for Administration appointed in Britain in 1967 has no power to order a remedy. The *Conseil d'Etat* is the ultimate appeal court in administrative justice, but it also has the role of advising the Government on the drafting of Bills and decrees.

THE POLICE

The French police is an institution which pre-dates the first U.S. State police force by at least two hundred years, and Paris was given a lieutenant-general of police by Louis XIV in 1667. Today there are several distinct police forces, but all are tightly controlled by the Minister of the Interior in Paris.

The national police force numbers about 50,000 and is distributed among the towns with 10,000 population and over and certain smaller ones. The nine regions into which the force is divided are controlled locally by an inspector-general and the central headquarters is the *Sûreté Nationale* headed, since a recent reform, by a secretary-general and forming part of the Ministry of the Interior.

The most familiar policeman to foreign visitors is presumed to be the *gendarme,* but strictly speaking he is a soldier, since the *gendarmerie* is part of the army. However, in addition to serving as the military police the *gendarmerie* is used to police the rural areas with a squad based in each canton. The *gendarmerie mobile,* distinguished by a red band on their caps or *képis,* can be rushed into towns to deal with emergencies but in holiday periods are being used increasingly to control road traffic. As a matter of interest the men seen controlling traffic in Paris and provincial towns are not gendarmes but *agents* or members of the municipal police.

A special riot police called *gardes mobiles* was established in 1921 to deal with the threat of political disturbances while the army was occupying the Rhineland. After the second world war the force was transformed into the para-military *Compagnie Républicaine de Securité,* known as the CRS, with its dark-blue battledress uniform; its first task was to deal with the wave of strikes organised by the Communists after being expelled from the government.

The CRS are greatly feared for the efficient methods of breaking up political demonstrations which they displayed during the disturbed period of the Algerian War, but since then their main task has been as highway police and, in an experiment which has proved successful, they are being used in holiday resorts to teach swimming and life-saving and to interest youth in physical fitness. All policemen carry arms, sometimes sub-machine guns, but the new uniform of the Paris *flic* or

' cop ' conceals his gun underneath his smart tunic. The familiar white baton is also disappearing. A folded cape is more effective in a riot, but raincoats have replaced the capes.

In Paris the police force comes under the authority of the Prefect of Police. The 26,000 members are divided between the uniformed municipal police who are responsible for public order and the control of traffic and the plain clothes *police judiciaire* who combat organised crime. Until recently the Paris Prefecture, although under the Minister of the Interior, enjoyed a large decree of autonomy, with the result that it overlapped in some cases the services of the *Sûreté Nationale*. The need for some reform was long recognised, but following the Ben Barka affair in 1965-6, in which some policemen were involved in the kidnapping and disappearance of the exiled Moroccan left-wing leader, General de Gaulle ordered an immediate reform. The result is a gradual merger between the Prefecture and the Sûreté.

Within the Sûreté and the Prefecture there are a number of specialised services such as the *Renseignements Généraux*, an intelligence branch which keeps an eye on foreigners, casinos, racetracks, political parties and clubs or associations, all of which have to be declared and registered. A much publicised ' anti-gang squad ' corresponds to the Scotland Yard Flying Squad and has a hard time keeping peace between rival gangs on the Riviera; counter-espionage within France is the responsibility of the *Direction de la Surveillance du Territoire*.

DEFENCE

The President of the Republic is the Commander-in-Chief of the armed forces and only he can order the nuclear striking force into action. He is assisted by the Council of Defence which consists of the Prime Minister and the ministers for Foreign Affairs, the Interior, the Armed Forces and, if called on, the Minister of Finance.

According to the Constitution the Prime Minister is responsible for national defence, but until 1969 this had been one of the

' reserved domains' under the direct supervision of General de Gaulle. The Minister of the Armed Forces, with authority over the Army, Navy and Air Force, carries out military policy. He is assisted by the Chief of Staff of the armed forces and the General Staffs of the three services.

The armed forces are now organised into three groups (1) the nuclear strategic force; (2) operational forces; (3) home defence forces. In 1966 the strength of the armed forces was estimated as Army—332,000; Navy—70,000; Air Force—110,000.

The nuclear strategic force consists of a first generation of sixty-two Mirage IV supersonic bombers armed with atomic bombs of an explosive force ranging from sixty to ninety kilotons. Fifty-one of these planes were in service early in 1967 and the rest were delivered by the end of the year. The second generation, which was supposed to be operational in 1971, will consist of medium-range ground-to-ground ballistic missiles armed with nuclear warheads. Construction of the launching silos in Upper Provence began in 1967.

The third generation is to consist of nuclear submarines armed with polaris-type missiles. The enriched uranium for the thermonuclear warheads is produced by the nuclear plant at Pierrelatte in the lower Rhône valley. The first submarine was launched in 1967 and three are expected to be in service before 1973. According to the defence equipment programme for the period 1965-70, the nuclear strategic force would absorb half the estimated £4,600 million budget.

The operational forces comprise Army, Navy and Air Force units ready to intervene immediately in case of attack. Two mechanised army divisions are based in West Germany but were withdrawn from NATO command, as were all other French forces, on 1 July 1966. Three more divisions are stationed in France, one of which is highly mobile and ready to fly overseas to Madagascar and the eleven former French territories in Africa with which France has defence agreements and where 6,000 troops are based at strategic points. The Air Force contribution is Mirage III interceptors, helicopters and transport planes and the Navy supplies aircraft carriers, frigates and numerous assault craft. Finally, the home defence forces, which also comprise the three services, are organised into seven military regions and twenty-one subdivisions. The 60,000 men of the *gendarmerie* have an important role in this sector.

All French males between eighteen and fifty are liable for national service, which comprises twelve months of active duty and eight periods of further obligations, none of which can exceed a month. The service can be accomplished in the armed forces or, in the case of those with special qualifications, as technical advisers, teachers or doctors in the overseas territories and former colonies. As the annual needs of the armed forces are estimated at 220,000 and the available intake is almost twice this number, a detailed scale of dispensations and deferments is used to match the supply with the demand. The Minister of the Armed Forces told Parliament in May 1967 that when the nuclear striking force was fully operational in 1974 its destructive power would be of the order of thirty megatons. Speaking about national service he said that ninety-five per cent of the conscripts accomplished military service and of the remaining five per cent 10,000 did a tour overseas under the heading of co-operation and the other 10,000 were given dispensations.

CURRENCY AND TAXATION

The basic currency unit is the *franc* of 100 *centimes*. In 1957 it was devalued by twenty per cent and in December 1958 by seventeen and a half per cent, so that the exchange rate became 1,382 francs to £1 (492.7 francs to one dollar). The 'new franc' worth one hundred old francs was introduced in January 1960, and in August 1969 another devaluation gave the rate of 5.5 francs to the dollar.

Although it is now more than ten years since the change, French people still mentally calculate in old francs, especially when talking about salaries, rents and prices. Newspapers frequently express amounts in old francs, adding the letters 'AF' standing for *anciens francs* although this practice is frowned on by the Government. Radio and television announcers try to avoid confusion by saying *francs lourds* or heavy francs to indicate the new unit.

The confusion is less troublesome for visitors and tourists now that most of the older notes and coins have been withdrawn. The most common notes in service are those for five, ten, fifty and a hundred francs. The coins are divided into five-franc and one-franc pieces and one, five, ten, twenty and fifty-centime pieces. There are also ten-franc silver coins, but they are rarely seen because pensioners, to whom they are distributed by priority, and the shopkeepers like to hoard them.

In 1967 the rigid exchange controls in force in France since the war were abolished for the most part and the franc was made fully convertible into all foreign currencies. Also restored was complete freedom to move gold in and out of the country. Unlike in the U.S. and Britain, anybody can buy gold in France, where it has always had a strong, even mystic, appeal for a peasantry too accustomed to inflation and successive devaluations to put much confidence in other savings. Following the May 1968 crisis, France's huge gold and foreign currency reserves fell from about $5.9 billion to $4 billion in several months and severe exchange controls were re-imposed to prevent the flight of capital abroad.

For revenue the French Government relies far more heavily on indirect taxation than any other developed country. In 1965, out of the total revenue of 97,693 million francs (approximately $19.5 billion, £7,100 million), personal income tax amounted to eighteen per cent (in the United States about sixty per cent of the total Internal Revenue taxes, in Britain thirty-seven per cent), company tax eight per cent and indirect taxes including customs and excise sixty-two per cent. Thus it is as consumers that the French pay the most taxes, and this system is often criticised, as by its very nature it is indiscriminate. The Government has had to resort to this method because of the fierce resistance to income tax shown by the French since it was instituted and the widespread practice of false declarations. Income tax based on annual declarations is paid in instalments.

Nevertheless revenue from income tax is steadily growing as more persons become eligible for payment and was almost ten times greater in 1967 than in 1952. More than half of French households are paying income tax now, compared to less than a quarter in 1950.

A survey made in 1966 by a London firm of industrial consultants of 'take-home' pay in various countries showed that French income tax was the lowest. The survey claimed that a married executive in France with two children and a gross income of $12,000 (£5,000) had a net income of $10,350 (£4,310) compared to $8,690 (£3,620) if he were living in Britain and $9,650 (£4,020) if he were in the United States.

This slight advantage for the French taxpayer seems to be heavily outweighed by the high rate of indirect taxation to which he is subjected. The most widespread of these taxes is the Added Value Tax which has now been adopted by the other Common Market countries and will presumably have to be adopted by Britain if she joins the EEC.

The AVT is a twenty per cent tax on sales at the production and wholesale levels collected in a series of fractional payments. The tax is levied by the Treasury at each stage but only on the value which each stage has added to the product. There are reduced rates for some products and increased rates for luxuries. In 1968 the AVT was extended to cover retail sales and commercial services and replace the local taxes which were mentioned in the section on local government. At the same time the general rate was reduced to sixteen per cent.

There is increasing criticism in France by the trade unions that the employees and workers on fixed salaries shoulder an unfair burden of the tax revenue, since the system of tax declarations for those in professional occupations, shopkeepers, artisans and other self-employed categories leaves the way open to excessive frauds. The quaint system of judging incomes by 'exterior signs of wealth' such as the kind of dog or car owned by a person is now less current but has not disappeared.

3

How They Live

HOUSING

IN spite of a massive building programme which has resulted in the construction of over four million homes since the war, the housing situation in France remains critical and it is even claimed that the French are the worst-housed people in Europe. Detailed analyses of the results of the census in 1962 are revealing in this respect.

Two-thirds of French homes were built before the first world war and one-third before 1871. In rural areas half the dwellings are more than a hundred years old and even in Paris more than half were built before 1914. Because of their age the sanitary facilities of a large proportion of French homes are primitive by modern standards. In 1962 almost a quarter had no running water, most of them, of course, in the country, but the figure for Paris was twelve per cent.

There was no interior water closet in sixty per cent of homes. In country areas the figure was eighty-one per cent and in Paris forty-three per cent. Eighty per cent of rural homes had neither bath, shower nor wash basin. For towns with more than 100,000 inhabitants the figure was fifty per cent and in Paris forty-three per cent.

The census established the total number of homes as 16,343,620. Of these five per cent were vacant and almost six

per cent were described as 'secondary residences.' A further
category called 'false homes' accounted for four per cent of
the total or 663,660 dwellings. These were makeshift structures,
hotel rooms, attics, cellars and various types of completely un-
suitable abodes for human beings. Even when the rooms were
reasonably well furnished they were often seriously overcrowded.

Again Paris was the worst affected and 271,300 homes were
described as belonging to this category. In the five years since the
census the figure is estimated to have risen to 280,000, so that
one person in five in the capital can be said to be badly housed.
Yet, paradoxically, in April 1967 there were sufficient new but
unsold apartments in the city and suburbs to house 50,000 people
and the number of unsold apartments in various stages of completion for the Paris area alone totalled the record figure of
46,143. For the whole country the number of unsold apartments was estimated at 150,000. The explanation was simply that
the building promoters, encouraged by the boom in expensive
housing early in the 1960s, when thousands of repatriates were
pouring back into France from North Africa, continued to cater
for a market that dried up fairly quickly. The fantastic jump
in prices for building land in Paris and the *Côte d'Azur* (about

In this Burgundy vineyard the wives and daughters help to
harvest the grapes which will be transformed into the celebrated Clos Vougeot wine. Unfortunately for the French
their wealth of vineyards is a real hazard for their health,
since more persons die in France of cirrhosis of the liver (32.8
per 100,000 inhabitants) than in any other European country.
Doctors blame excessive wine drinking, as 2 million French
people drink two litres (0.4 gallons) a day and 4.6 million
drink at least one litre.

The time when distinguished English visitors 'discovered'
the beauties of the Mediterranean coastline, unknown to most
of the French, is long past, although Nice, Monte Carlo and
Cannes reveal many traces of the Victorian era. The little
fishing village of St Tropez (opposite) sees its population of
6,000 swell to 60,000 every August.

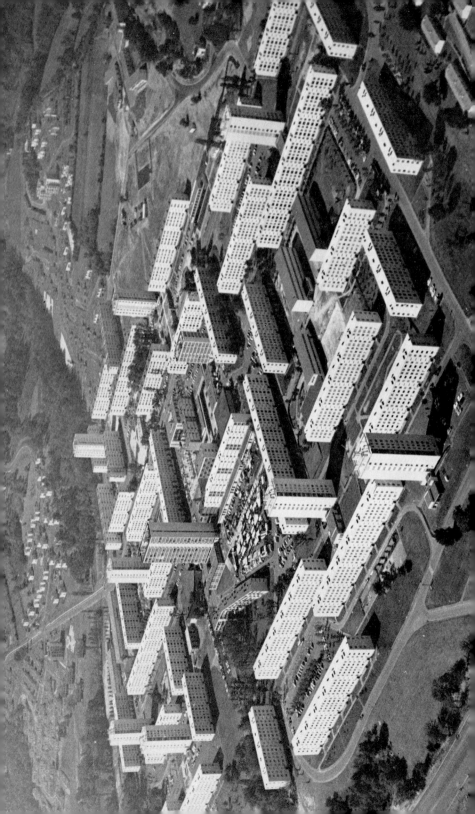

1,000 per cent between 1950 and 1964) forced the speculators to keep their prices high and the Government's hope that scarcity of buyers would force them down has so far been in vain.

The situation in 1967 was summed up thus in *Le Monde* by M Gilbert Mathieu, an authority on French housing: 'While almost one French person in four lives in an overcrowded apartment, while two out of three homes date from before 1914 and while one-third of young households do not live in normal conditions, the nation allows its construction to stagnate.'

To understand the housing crisis in France and appreciate what is being done a brief look should be given to its origins. Firstly, at the beginning of the first world war there was the unwise freezing of rents which is still in operation, though on a reduced scale. The result of this policy was that between the wars there was no incentive for private investment in new housing and more homes are now built in one year in France than were built in the whole period from 1914 to 1947. Because of the fall in population in the inter-war years the effects of this stagnation were not readily apparent.

Northern France suffered severely in both world wars and in the second alone 450,000 homes were completely destroyed and

———

The general flight from the rural areas to the cities and towns has been reversed in a few cases such as Mourenx in the Pyrenees. Here a village of 200 people has been transformed into this modern, well laid-out town built for the families of the workers employed at Lacq, a few miles away, where oil and gas have been discovered since the war. The contrast with the nineteenth-century coal-mining towns in the north of France and England is striking.

almost two million damaged. Consequently the immediate post-war years were taken up with the work of reconstruction, and the housing programme proper only began moving forward again in 1948 after a nine-year interruption.

But now another factor intervened to make the situation more serious. As we have seen, the population after the war began to increase at a totally unexpected rate and this only heightened the inadequacy of the existing housing. The full effect of the demographic bound forward will only become evident between 1970 and 1980 as the young French people born in the record baby-boom years after 1946 go house-hunting. The flight from the land to the urban areas plus the influx of immigrant workers are also contributing to the rush for urban accommodation that does not yet exist.

Successive governments have tried with partial success to solve the housing problem. The rent freeze has been abolished for dwellings constructed since the war and is being slowly relaxed on the older ones, especially the more luxurious kind. Although these measures have encouraged private investment they have also resulted in two serious disadvantages. The first has been noted, namely over-concentration on expensive apartments. The second is that rents are unjustifiably divided into two categories, one excessively high and the other unrealistically low.

The 1962 census showed that of the 14.5 million main dwellings, about six million were owned and 8.5 million rented. Approximately six million tenants were, however, living in rent-controlled dwellings, which meant they had a considerable financial advantage. In Paris, for example, a young married couple renting a new three-room flat would pay between $36 (£15) and $60 (£25) a week, depending on the area, while their parents might be paying as little as $12 (£5) a week in an older but more spacious apartment. If the couple wanted to buy a flat in Paris for, say, $19,000 (£8,000) which is somewhat below the average, according to the estimate by the president of a building promoters' association, the most favourable credit terms obtainable were $5,500 (£2,300) down and monthly payments of $144 (£60) over twelve years. Such terms were impossible for

the majority of badly-housed families whose average income
was $275 (£115) a month.

New cheap housing does exist in France for the lower income
groups and government aid is being increasingly concentrated
on this sector, but the supply is by far inferior to the demand
and until the 1970s the situation will probably get worse before it
improves. These *habitations à loyer moderé* (HLM) or medium-
rent houses are the equivalent of council flats in Britain and are
especially conspicuous in the Paris suburbs, where in blocks ten
to fifteen storeys high they tower over the drab little houses
(*pavillons*) that until the war characterised French suburbia.

The construction of the HLM is financed by four types of
organisation, official and private, which in turn are financed
by long-term State loans of up to fifty years at one per cent
interest. About three-quarters of HLM built are for letting at
low rents and the rest are for owner-occupiers who accede to full
ownership over a fixed period of years. In theory only families
whose incomes do not exceed a certain ceiling are eligible for
HLM and the waiting list grows every month. In 1966 the State
subsidised the beginning of construction of 157,000 HLM and in
the same year about 130,000 were completed. Employers are
obliged by law to invest a sum equivalent to ten per cent of their
wage bill in housing for lower income groups, but as only the
very large nationalised concerns like the Coal Board can actually
build houses for their employees, the majority of contributions
are diverted to the HLM programme. The social benefits for
poorer families include a rent allowance for which over one
million families qualified in 1966. A family with two children
having an income of $44 (£18) a week and a rent of $15 (£6)
a week would receive a rent allowance of about $9 (£3 15s).

A more extensive method of government aid for housing is
provided by the State bank *Crédit Foncier*, which lends money
at five per cent over twenty years. About four-fifths of French
families can in theory benefit from these loans, which are limited
to owner-occupiers or proprietors who guarantee to charge a
rent not exceeding a limit fixed by the Government. In practice,
however, the bank's loans only cover forty to sixty per cent of

the construction price and the terms at which the rest of the money would have to be raised from private sources are so unfavourable that few working-class families could afford it.

The size of the *Crédit Foncier*'s loans vary according to the type of home being bought and the size of the family. For example, a couple with one child buying a three-room flat (not including the kitchen) would get about $6,000 (£2,500) repayable over twenty years at five per cent. Persons who do not seek loans from the State can qualify for non-repayable grants. Again for a three-room flat this could amount to $108 (£45) a year over ten years or $67 (£28) over twenty years. In 1966, out of the total number of 413,000 homes completed, 121,000 benefited from *Crédit Foncier* loans and 77,000 from grants. Almost ninety per cent of homes built in France benefit from State loans or grants, compared with forty-five per cent in Britain and two per cent in the United States.

In the same year in the private sector 79,000 homes were completed, which was twice as many as in 1964. Up to the present mortgages for longer than ten years have been extremely difficult to get. The Bank of France loans were fixed at ten years at ten per cent and some notaries would advance three-year loans against mortgages but at rates of ten to fifteen per cent. In 1967 the Government urged the banks, the largest of which are nationalised, to give mortgages on more favourable terms and this policy immediately began to bear fruit, as in the face of unaccustomed competition some banks were offering twenty-year loans at eight per cent.

The increasing affluence of the executive and professional classes in recent years has been finding an outlet in the rush for apartments classed as ' grand standing ' in the choice residential areas of towns or the fashionable outskirts. In Paris the phenomenon has been especially noticeable in the country west and south of the capital, near the motorways. The trend is towards ' residences ' or clusters of apartment blocks served by their own shopping centres, swimming pools, night clubs and cinemas. For the project near Versailles called ' Parly 2 ' (originally Paris-2 but changed on the order of the indignant Paris municipal council) it was planned to build 5,000 luxury flats by 1970. One thousand flats were claimed to have been sold at prices ranging from $12,500 (£5,200) for a three-room type to $53,000 (£22,000) for a six-room type within a few weeks of the first advertisements, before the foundations were even laid.

Although the average French family, unlike its British or American counterpart, takes it for granted that home is a flat and not a two-storey house with a garden front and back, in recent years there has been a spectacular increase in ' weekend houses,' which for Parisians means converted farmhouses, bungalows or even châteaux in the countryside, anything up to a hundred miles from the capital. According to the 1962 census there were 951,000 secondary residences, most of them in the Paris region, the *Côte d'Azur*, the Alps, the Loire Valley and Brittany. In 1965 the number had increased to 1.25 million or three times more than in 1954.

Compared to the rest of Europe, France occupies a medium position as regards housing. The figures published by the United Nations Commission in Geneva for 1965 show that France, with 8.4 homes completed per thousand inhabitants, had climbed from eleventh to eighth place in the European housing league. Sweden was first with 12.5.

Under the Fifth National Plan for 1966-70 France's housing programme was intended to reach the target of 470,000 homes a year in 1970, but this was later raised to 500,000 to take into account the unexpected increase in population.

MODERN CONVENIENCES

Few French households have domestic servants and, even if financial reasons were not an obstacle in certain cases, space would be, as the average flat has not the luxury of a spare room. At the beginning of 1965 the number of people in domestic service was estimated at 478,000 for approximately fifteen million households, so less than one housewife in thirty had a full-time maid. These figures do not indicate how many homes are using *au pair* girls for domestic work, but the number must be substantial in the Paris area, where thousands of girls studying French at the *Alliance Française* and other language institutes do domestic work to pay their way.

Since the war there have been significant changes in the spending habits of French households, but nowhere have they been more striking than under the heading of *habitation* which is subdivided into (a) *logement* including rent or mortgage and rates, (b) equipment and (c) energy, meaning gas, electricity and heating. If one hundred is taken as the index for 1949, by 1959 the consumption indices for the three headings at current prices were (a) 518, (b) 399 and (c) 296. Between 1959 and 1965, taking one hundred as the base index for 1959, the consumption indices at current prices in 1965 were (a) 226, (b) 158 and (c) 156.

Total spending by French households in 1959 came to 167,627 million francs (about $33.5 billion, £12,280 million) and the proportion allotted to *habitation* was 16.4 per cent. In 1965 total consumption at current prices had risen to 284,198 million francs (about $57 billion, £20,819 million) and the percentage for *habitation* to 17.3. Finally, calculating spending on homes at constant prices (1959), the increase between 1959 and 1965 was forty-three per cent but at current prices seventy-nine per cent.

Although French homes, by British or American standards, do not seem impressively equipped with modern conveniences, the most significant factor seems to be less the state of being under-equipped than the progress made over the past decade, as the following table shows.

Percentage of French homes having modern conveniences

	1954	1966
Refrigerator	7.5	64
Washing machine	8.4	44
Vacuum cleaner	14	47
Radio	72	85
Television	1	52
Record player	unknown	33
Car	21	51

These home comforts are distributed, of course, in varying

proportions according to the social categories, with the professional and executive classes the most favoured, since in January 1965 ninety-one per cent of these homes had a refrigerator, sixty-two per cent a washing machine, eighty-nine per cent a vacuum cleaner, sixty per cent a television set, seventy-five per cent a record player and eighty-seven per cent a car.

It is, however, worth noting how rapidly the lower income groups are rising up the scale of symbols of the affluent society, a factor all the more interesting in France because a large proportion of these homes regularly vote Communist.

Percentage of homes of manual workers (a) and farm labourers (b) having modern conveniences

	(a)		(b)	
	1954	1965	1954	1965
Refrigerator	3.3	53.4	0.5	32.4
Washing machine	8.5	44.4	1.8	32.9
Vacuum cleaner	6.3	40.1	1.0	8.1
Television	0.9	44.3	unknown	20.2
Record player	unknown	30.4	unknown	20.1
Car	8.0	42.4	3.0	34.1

For such a highly developed country the number of telephones in France is surprisingly small. In 1965 there were 124 phones per 1,000 inhabitants compared to 188 in Britain and 478 in the United States. Pets are hardly modern conveniences but it is interesting to note that one in every three French homes has a pet of some kind, usually a cat or a dog. A survey made recently revealed that these pets include 5,000 reptiles of all descriptions and 20,000 monkeys; there are also several crocodiles, lions and tigers. The consumers' magazine which published the survey claimed that in Britain one home in five had a pet and in the United States only one in forty.

WHAT THEY EAT AND DRINK

Strange as it may appear, food and drink are becoming less important to the French every year. In 1950 half the family

budget was spent on nourishment but by 1963 the proportion
had fallen steadily to thirty-eight per cent (35.5 per cent in
Britain, 24.6 per cent in the United States) while the shares of
housing, health, transport and leisure had substantially increased.
In spite of the change of emphasis, revolutionary given the
French background, the actual amount spent on food and drink
increases each year, even allowing for the increased population
and rising prices.

In 1964 total French spending on all goods and services was
268,778 million francs (about $54 billion, £19,500 million).
Breaking this down, it appears that an average French household
spent $3,565 (£1,320) in the year or $297 (£110) a month. This
figure represents a real increase in the standard of living of
eighty per cent over fifteen years.

It is interesting to compare the evolution of annual spending
per head in France with other European countries and the
United States between 1950 and 1963.

Country	1950	1963
France	100	100
Britain	131	105
Italy	54	60
West Germany	83	109
Holland	92	82
Belgium	124	93
United States	250	186

Getting back to food and drink, in 1963 the French spent
96,386 million francs on them (about $20 billion, £7,000
million). The biggest items were meat which accounted for more
than a quarter of the total, drink which accounted for a fifth,
and cereals which were slightly more than a tenth compared to
fourteen per cent in 1950. Fruit and vegetables together came
to thirteen per cent and milk and cheese to eight per cent.

The increasing popularity of meat is noteworthy, since annual
consumption per head has grown, from twenty-eight kilogrammes
(61.7 lb) in 1950 to thirty-seven kilogrammes (81.5 lb) in 1963
in spite of an annual price increase of 3.3 per cent. The con-

sumption of pork has doubled in twelve years, chiefly perhaps because it is cheaper than beef. Horse meat has also become more popular, but it is now almost as dear as beef. Lamb has moved into the luxury bracket.

Annual bread consumption per head over the same period, 1950-63, has fallen from 282 lb to 220 lb and potatoes from 273 lb to 231 lb. Fresh fruit consumption has risen from 80 lb to 125 lb; fresh fish from 16 lb to 24 lb; cheese from 19 lb to 31 lb; butter from 18 lb to 23 lb and sugar from 31 lb to 42 lb. Significant increases in tinned foods reflect the changes in traditional French *cuisine* which foreigners seem to bemoan more than the French themselves.

The daily diet of the Frenchman varies considerably according to his social status and even the region he lives in. Thus a farm worker spends on average $26 (£11) a year on bread while an executive spends only $14 (£6). The latter's expenditure on meat is $74 (£31), the farm worker's less than half that. The annual average consumption of potatoes per person is 203 lb (1965) but for the working-class it rises to 242 lb and for the executive grades falls to 132 lb. The record is held by the Nord department where annual consumption of potatoes is 385 lb per person.

Under the heading of drink the French still consume a staggering amount of wine. The annual consumption of cheap wine for persons over fourteen years of age in 1963 was thirty-four gallons plus another two gallons of quality wines. In Britain the average is about a half a gallon. The new affluence in France can be seen from the fact that between 1950 and 1963 the sale of quality wines more than doubled while that of ordinary wine increased by about fifteen per cent. Non-alcoholic drinks are in a small way beginning to replace *vin ordinaire* at meals, although it is impossible to know to what extent this is due to government-sponsored campaigns in favour of sobriety. In the period we have been considering the annual per capita consumption of mineral water almost tripled to 5.5 gallons.

The actual meals in a French home when guests are not being entertained are simpler than a foreigner might think.

Breakfast, as everyone knows, consists of coffee and rolls called *croissants* or more commonly merely bread, butter and jam. Why the French should be so unimaginative about breakfast is a mystery. Children may be given orange juice, cornflakes and an egg. After such meagre fare it is not surprising that lunch has to be substantial. A typical one would begin with a plate of raw vegetables (*crudités*) such as carrots, beetroot and cucumber or else a slice of *paté* made of goose liver. Next a main course of beef, veal or pork. The average household would find the price of good meat prohibitive for everyday consumption however, and stews from the cheaper cuts and chicken are common. Salad, cheese and fruit will end the meal, which is usually put down with a cup of black coffee.

Afternoon tea or 'elevenses' are virtually unknown, at least in offices and factories. Housewives out shopping in the afternoon will often pop into a *salon du thé* for a refreshing cup of lemon tea. In the evening dinner is eaten between seven-thirty and nine-thirty. The first course will often be soup and the other courses follow the lunch pattern.

The staple and best loved French dish is *bifteck frites* or plain steak (literally bloody) and chips washed down with red wine. The famous snails and frogs' legs are not a myth, but most Frenchmen would trade them for a steak any day.

CLOTHES

The French spend about twelve per cent of their budget on clothes and this figure remains more or less constant although the price of clothes compared to other goods has been diminishing. In 1964 total spending on clothes was about 31,000 million francs, ($6.2 billion, £2,250 million). Slightly less than half this was spent on garments proper, the sales of which seem to follow closely the rate of increase in per capita incomes. On the other hand hats have become increasingly popular, perhaps as Frenchmen stop wearing berets, and sales are increasing at about eighteen per cent annually. A new impetus in the sale of shoes has also been observed since 1959.

In subsequent sections we shall consider in more detail how the French amuse themselves and get about. The following table shows the relative importance of their various spending in 1965.

Total consumption 284,198 million francs (about $57 billion, £20,819 million).

	per cent
Food and drink	33
Clothes	10
Shoes	1.7
Housing and equipment	17.3
Health and hygiene	12
Transport, telephone and post	8.7
Culture and leisure	7
Hotels, restaurants and varia	10.3
Total	100.0

WELFARE SERVICES

The post-war provisional government in 1945-6 introduced the social security system which is the equivalent of the welfare state in Britain, although there are important differences, especially in the health services. The existing legislation for the insurance and protection of wage-earners was grouped together and extended while being brought under a single organisation which was to administer the system throughout the country under the control of the Ministry of Social Affairs. Side by side with the social security system the traditional privately-run friendly societies dating back to the nineteenth century have continued to exist, and their number is estimated at 20,000, catering for fifteen million members.

Until 1967 the social security code covered all wage-earners and salaried persons as well as their families, but did not extend to self-employed persons. In 1966 legislation was passed extending the system to this last category and it was brought into force in 1967, so virtually the whole population including foreign workers now benefit from it. Other changes introduced under decree legislation towards the end of 1967 to remedy the system's growing deficit will be considered later.

The system is self-financed by employers' and workers' contributions, not at a flat rate as in Britain, but as a percentage of salaries. Until the 1967 reform the employer paid fifteen per cent and the employee six per cent, but where the monthly salary exceeded 1,140 francs (about $228, £83), the contributions were made only on the basis of that sum. The employee's share is deducted at source. The benefits include medical insurance, pensions, death benefits, family allowances and insurance for accidents at work which will be treated in the next chapter.

HEALTH INSURANCE

Under the French system free medical treatment is not directly provided by the State but insured persons are reimbursed by the social security for a varying percentage of their expenses. There are no doctors' lists as in Britain and people are free to choose their own doctor and dentist. In this way it is believed the tradition of ' liberal medicine ' is preserved, but in practice the State's intervention in the health services is becoming more and more important.

The question of fees, for example, is ruled by a decree made in 1960. This laid down that where agreements (*conventions*) could not be reached between the social security and the doctors' and dentists' associations in the different departments, a government commission would fix fees to which individual practitioners could adhere. The situation now is that if a doctor or dentist is *conventionné*, and most of them are, the social security reimburses up to eighty per cent of his fee, but considerably less than this if he has not agreed to the scale of fees laid down by the Government. The doctors' and dentists' associations are not very happy with this arrangement as they feel the fees fixed are too low—in Paris in 1967, $3 (24s) for an ordinary consultation, about $5 (37s) for a visit at home. On the other hand, if a doctor does not accept the fixed fee he risks losing those patients who want to be reimbursed at the maximum rate.

Drugs prescribed by a doctor are reimbursed at between seventy and ninety per cent if they are on the list approved by the social security. The repayment is made within a short period by the local social security *caisse* or fund which is administered by boards representing employers and employees and elected at fixed intervals. At a higher level are sixteen regional *caisses* to co-ordinate policy and at the top a national *caisse* which controls the distribution of funds. Informal arrangements can sometimes be made with doctors and chemists enabling them to be reimbursed directly, with the patient merely paying the outstanding amount. In addition many persons can supplement the social security payment through belonging to a friendly society or through a special fund financed by their employers. This is often the case with large firms and the semi-state industries like mining, railways, gas and electricity. Treatment is entirely free in the case of serious operations and certain illnesses.

Hospitals in France are either public (*assistance publique*) and run by the local authorities, or private. In the case of the former, reimbursement by the social security is direct and for the latter in accordance with a scale of fees as with the *conventionné* doctors and dentists.

A World Health Organisation report published in 1966 gave the following statistics for French hospital facilities.

Institution	Beds
Public hospitals	201,000
Private hospitals and rest homes	67,000
Old persons' homes (public)	200,000
Old persons' homes (private)	73,000
Anti-tuberculosis sanatoriums	70,800
Mental hospitals	100,000
Anti-cancer centres	2,950
Children's hospitals	33,700
Readaptation centres	5,500
Others	2,000

The total of 755,950 beds worked out at sixteen per 1,000 inhabitants or eleven if the old persons' homes are left out of account. The WHO noted that in general this situation compared favourably with other European countries such as Italy and Germany and taking into account that in France medical treatment at home was usual except in serious cases. In mental hospitals and old persons' homes, however, the equipment was still insufficient for the needs, the report noted. Under the Fifth National Plan for the period 1966-70 the Government proposed to increase the number of beds by 100,000 (critics estimate that three times this number are needed) and modernise about the same number, but the credits released for this ambitious programme seemed to be inadequate.

At the end of 1964 there were 54,964 physicians, 15,757 pharmacists and 17,746 dentists practising in France. In 1962 it was estimated that there was one doctor for every 887 inhabitants compared with one for 930 in Britain and for 762 in the United States. On the other hand it was pointed out that French hospital equipment would be altogether inadequate for the needs of a national health service on the British model. At present there is a serious shortage of qualified nurses in public hospitals, where the pay and working conditions are unattractive. Male and female nurses at the end of 1964 totalled 121,820 and registered midwives 8,530.

According to social security statistics, in 1962 252,804 persons received medical treatment for a period longer than six months. Tuberculosis accounted for twenty per cent of these. About 38,000 were treated for cancer and the same number for nervous disorders; heart ailments accounted for 16,000, digestive disorders 14,000 and arthritis and rheumatism 14,000.

Deaths in 1964 totalled 516,478. The principal causes were heart ailments (97,600), cancer (95,300), old age and unknown (71,400), cerebral damage (62,400), accidents including road deaths (32,700).

FAMILY ALLOWANCES

Certain family allowances have been compulsory in France

since 1932 but now they are grouped under the social security code and administered by a *caisse* which may be separate from that dealing with medical benefits or combined with it as in the Paris region and most of the departments. The fund is financed by employers' contributions only and, unlike medical insurance, family allowances have since 1945 extended to everybody, including the self-employed.

There are six different allowances, regulated according to a basic monthly salary which in Paris was fixed at 328 francs ($65, £27 7s) in December 1967.

(1) Pre-natal allowances for which all pregnant women are eligible and in 1967 amounting to $14.5 (£6) a month over nine months.

(2) Maternity allowance of $132 (£54 13s) payable after birth.

In addition to these allowances an expectant mother who is also a wage-earner is usually given full pay during the fourteen weeks' permitted absence from work.

(3) Children's allowances are calculated at twenty-two per cent of the basic salary for the second child and thirty-three per cent for the third and subsequent children. Increases are given for children over ten and fifteen. Health insurance, which formerly extended only to children under sixteen, is now extended to children from sixteen to eighteen if apprentices and from seventeen to twenty if studying.

(4) The allowance for a non-working mother is calculated on a basic monthly salary of about $41 (£17) and amounts to twenty per cent for one child, forty per cent for two and fifty per cent for three or more children.

(5) Housing allowance calculated according to rent, size of family and salary.

(6) In 1963 a special allowance was introduced to help pay for the specialised education required for handicapped children.

There is a widespread impression abroad that French families virtually live off the proceeds of their various allowances. The results of an extremely thorough survey conducted over a year, published in 1967, gave the following information : in 1962-3 the total annual resources of the average family, that is salaries, over-

time and allowances, was 18,900 francs ($3,800, £1,390) but
for half the families studied the figure was 16,700 francs ($3,350,
£1,220). Family allowances represented eleven per cent of
resources in families with two children, and thirty-seven per cent
in families with six children. In larger families, half their
resources came from allowances when the former totalled less
than 17,200 francs, ($3,450, £1,260). It is estimated that only
in the larger and poorer families do the allowances actually cover
the cost of rearing the children. The average cost of a child is
reckoned at 1,500 francs ($300, £110) a year, of which slighly
less than half is spent on nourishment. It is admitted, however,
that for the average middle-class family, especially in Paris, the
' cost of a child ' is much higher than this figure.

CARE OF THE OLD

The considerable number of old people in France poses a
serious problem, for the State is committed to providing them
with an adequate means of existence. In 1965 the number of
persons over sixty-five years of age was 5.5 million or 11.6 per
cent of the population. A government commission set up in 1961

––––––

One of France's best known trains, the Mistral express linking
Paris with the Riviera, on its daily run up the Rhône valley.
The line is fully electrified and the train reaches speeds of
over 100 mph on some stretches.

A half-size version of the experimental aerotrain being tested
near Paris. By using a rocket for extra acceleration the train's
cruising speed of 125 mph was boosted to 188 mph. The full-
size version of the aerotrain will carry about eighty passengers
and its designer, M Bertin, claims it could travel at 250 mph
on long runs. Experiments are to be made on a noiseless
version of the aerotrain, using an electric ' linear ' engine.

to study ways of improving the lot of old persons recommended that by 1965 they should be assured of a minimum annual sum of 2,200 francs ($440, £160). This target was accepted, but was not reached until the end of 1967.

Pensions for insured persons depend on the average salary (up to a fixed ceiling) over the ten years before retirement and on how long the person was insured. To qualify for the normal pension a person must have been making insurance payments for thirty years. If retirement takes place at sixty, the pension is twenty per cent of the basic salary, but is increased by four per cent for every year worked after sixty. In cases of distress or insufficient means an additional pension of $137 (£57) a year may be obtained from the organisation called the *Fonds National de Solidarité*. The higher-paid skilled workers, *cadres* and professions have their own special retirement and superannuation schemes as in Britain and the United States.

Other benefits for old persons include a housing allowance equal to three-quarters of their rent when their total resources do not exceed about $600 (£250) a year, and the right to up to thirty hours a month of home help.

A considerable effort is being made to increase and modernise

———

The longest bridge in France links the mainland with the island of Oléron, one-and-a-half miles off the west coast. It was built with pre-stressed concrete units.

the institutions for old persons who have no home of their own. The old fashioned Dickensian *hospices* are being slowly replaced by bright and comfortable homes called *maisons de retraite*. A formula which has proved successful is the *logement-foyer* in which individual flats are combined with communal restaurants and recreation facilities. More ambitious still are the experiments with whole villages specially designed for old persons in the sunniest parts of France. These villages are not isolated but are built on the outskirts of existing ones so that the old people can gradually become assimilated into the life of the region through daily contacts with the local inhabitants.

Behind the apparently satisfactory working of the social security system lies the shadow of an immense deficit, estimated in 1967 to be three thousand million francs or $600 million (£250 million) and at that rate likely to reach about $2 billion (£800 million) by 1970 unless a remedy were found. The reasons for the deficit were the rising cost of drugs and medical treatment, the transfer to the *régime ordinaire,* which was barely balancing its budget, of the deficits of the special régimes, especially the agricultural sector. Finally, the contributions of the insured persons were clearly being kept at an artificially low level in the case of those whose resources exceeded the basic salary by which the charges were calculated.

The following is a brief summary of the financial and administrative reforms introduced by the Government in the second half of 1967 to remedy the deficit. The changes, incidentally, were strongly opposed by most of the trade unions.

For employees, contributions were increased from six to six and a half per cent of the basic salary of 1,205 francs a month ($240, £100) and those earning more than that pay an additional one per cent on the excess. The employers' contributions were increased from fifteen to seventeen per cent of the basic salary and an extra two per cent was levied on the sum in excess of the basic salary which is adjusted each year. The new charges on employers were offset slightly by a reduction in their contributions towards family allowances which now amount to 11.5 per cent of the basic salary. Another economy was the decision to reduce from eighty to seventy per cent the coverage of medical and dental expenses by social security. To discourage abuses, persons who supplement the social security scheme by private health insurance will still have to pay five per cent. The medical expenses due to road accidents are no longer borne by the social security but by a fund financed by a special premium on motorists' insurance policies.

The administrative reforms include the setting up of three separate boards for sickness and maternity, old age pensions and family allowances. Each board will be responsible for its own budget.

4

How They Work

IN 1945 France's economy was in a desperate plight. Even before
the war short-sighted policies had left her lagging far behind the
other industrialised countries of Europe and in 1938 the industrial production index had fallen to the 1911 level and
exports were below the 1913 level. Machinery was on average
three times older than in Britain and the French worker had
only one-third of the mechanised power available to the British
worker. This already critical situation was made catastrophic as
a result of the devastation of the industrial areas wrought by the
war and the first efforts to recover were handicapped by the
extensive damage to roads, railways and bridges. In 1946 the
industrial production index was the same as in 1907.

Twenty years later, in the mid-sixties, all had changed; the
French ' economic miracle ' was a reality and France had become
one of the most prosperous countries in the world. Comparative
statistics of the Organisation for Economic Co-operation and
Development showed that *per capita* gross national product in
1965 in France was 1,920 dollars, slightly exceeding the figure
for Britain and West Germany although, of course, well below
that of the United States which was 3,560 dollars. France's
official holdings of gold and foreign exchange had by April
1968 risen to the impressive total of 5,900 million dollars.

The flight from the franc in the months following the May crisis was due more to speculation on the revaluation of the German mark than to any basic weakness in the French economy.

Further details of this spectacular economic recovery in the two decades following the war will emerge in the course of this chapter, but here we can consider briefly its explanation. First there was the country's wealth of natural resources, particularly in agriculture but also in minerals and sources of energy such as hydro-electric power and natural gas. Secondly the French engineering genius performed miracles with the crippled communications system and the devastated industrial areas in the north and east, and thirdly there was the generous and vital American aid programme culminating in the Marshall Plan. Yet all these factors could not have resulted in such a successful recovery, especially in view of the fact that France was engaged in continuous and costly colonial wars and was the prey to notorious political instability until 1958, if there had not been a co-ordinated reconstruction and modernisation policy. There was such a policy and it was called the National Plan.

The first plan covered the years 1947-53 and was called the Monnet Plan after its originator M Jean Monnet. It concentrated on the development of six basic industries: coal, electricity, transport, steel, cement and agricultural machinery. The targets set had been reached by 1952 and the second plan for 1954-7 switched attention from the basic industries to the improvement of agriculture, the modernisation of industry, housing, external trade and living standards. Expansion went on at such a rapid rate in this period that it provoked inflation and the Government had to introduce severe austerity measures at the beginning of the third plan (1958-61), including a seventeen per cent devaluation.

The fourth plan (1962-5) represented a change in emphasis by setting targets for social as well as economic development and the fifth plan (1965-70) continues this trend. The annual rate of economic expansion is fixed at five per cent, which means that total production should increase for that period by 93,000 million francs (almost $19 billion, £7,000 million). Two-thirds of this increase will be accounted for by an annual rise in per capita domestic consumption of 3.5 per cent; the remainder will be divided more or less equally between productive investment and social improvements such as housing, schools, health, roads and communications.

The success of French planning has attracted much interest abroad, particularly in Britain where a national plan was tentatively drawn up in 1966, only to be pushed into the background by the sterling crisis and the subsequent austerity measures.

The French planning machinery consists essentially of a permanent commissariat now under the authority of the Minister for Regional Development and the Plan and headed by a commissioner assisted by a relatively small team of civil servants. Their job is to frame policy and their decisions are based on the work of the modernisation committees appointed from the various sectors of the economy and representing all interests, government, industry, agriculture and trade unions. The commissariat supervises the work of the committees which can number as many as thirty and group more than a thousand persons. When the targets have been agreed upon, the government and a representative body called the Social and Economic Council study them and the latter may suggest amendments. Finally the plan is submitted to Parliament.

Once adopted, the plan is not binding as far as private enterprise is concerned and the commissariat has no powers to enforce its targets. In the public sector the government, of course, can insist that the nationalised industries follow the guidelines and as a rule the annual budget is drawn up in accordance with the investment targets of the current plan. There are various methods whereby the government can bring pressure on the private sector to follow the plan's recommendations, but on the whole the various plans have been a genuinely co-operative effort between all the interested parties.

Direct State control over the economy is more extensive in France than in Britain or the United States because of the relatively large number of nationalised industries and services.

This situation is the result of historical as well as doctrinaire causes and in fact the notion of state enterprise goes back as far as the seventeenth century, when Louis XIV nationalised the Gobelins tapestry works. The tobacco monopoly was established early in the nineteenth century with the result that the State is the sole purchaser of the crop, grown mainly in France itself, and cigarettes are made in State factories and sold by 50,000 concessionaires, usually cafés, called *tabacs* and marked outside by a red cigar sign. In return for commission on tobacco sales the *tabacs* are obliged to sell stamps—a useful tip for tourists which can save much time wasted looking for a post office.

Public enterprise in France today employs thirteen per cent of the active population and comprises the entire railway system, virtually all the fuel and energy resources, majority holdings in air and sea transport and the aviation industry, and one-third of both the automobile and the house-building industries. In addition sixty per cent of deposit bank business and one-third of insurance is handled by nationalised concerns. Most of this State takeover programme dates from the Popular Front socialist government of 1936 and to an even greater extent from the immediate post-war period when, inspired by the social charter of the wartime National Resistance Council, the preamble of the Fourth Republic Constitution laid down that ' every enterprise, the exploitation of which has or acquires the character of a national public service or a monopoly, must become the property of the Community.' In addition firms which were accused of collaboration with the Germans during the occupation were also taken over, notably the Renault motor works, the Agence Havas news agency and several newspaper plants.

The extent to which publicly-owned companies come under direct State control varies considerably and the managements of Air France and Renault, which do not enjoy a monopoly, are freer than, for example, the national railways board. The bigger nationalised concerns in France are, like those in other countries, plagued with growing deficits. In 1967 the Government had to raise fares and tariffs to find the money to subsidise the deficits of the Paris Metro, the gas and electricity industries and the railways.

MAIN INDUSTRIES

Not surprisingly the top industrial concerns in France, judged by capital and business turnover, are the State-owned monopolies of electricity, Paris transport, coal, tobacco, gas and the railways. It is interesting to note that in the list published in 1967 by the High Authority of the Coal and Steel Community of the ninety biggest companies in the Common Market and Britain, Electricité de France is the only French one in the 'top ten' and indeed occupies tenth place. Britain has three companies in this upper bracket; British Petroleum (3), National Coal Board (5) and Imperial Chemical Industries (7). The other places are filled by Royal Dutch/Shell (1), Unilever (2), IRI of Italy (4), Volkswagen (6), Philips (8) and Siemens (9). Out of the total of ninety, Britain and France each account for eighteen and West Germany forty-one.

Steel and iron is the principal non-nationalised heavy industry in France, employing about 220,000 workers. France ranks as the sixth biggest producer in the world after the United States, Russia, Japan, West Germany and Britain. Steel output in 1964 was 19.7 million tons compared to 6.1 million tons in 1938, and under the fifth plan it is expected to rise to 23.5 million tons by 1970. Originally the target was higher, but increased world competition is making itself felt. Also the iron ore deposits concentrated in Lorraine are of inferior quality to the ore furnished by former African colonies, and the consequent closing of the least productive mines is causing serious unemployment in eastern France.

Usinor, one of the biggest steel companies with a turnover in 1965 of almost $400 million (£150 million), has set up its most modern plant at Dunkirk to process ore from overseas. Iron ore output in France fell from 67 million tons in 1960 to 59.5 million tons in 1965 and the number of miners by over 6,000. At present the Government is trying to speed up the redistribution of redundant miners to other industries but progress is slow.

The mechanical and electrical industries as a group have the biggest turnover in the economy. The annual rate of growth for the group, which employs over 1.5 million persons, was 6.8 per cent between 1960 and 1965, but in some sector the percentage was much higher, such as household equipment (12.8), electronics (13.1) and electrical equipment (14.7). The Compagnie Générale d'Electricité is one of the biggest employers in the country, with 52,000 people on its payroll. French electrical equipment has several world-beating achievements to its credit including the fastest electric locomotives; 735,000-volt circuit-breakers; a 600,000-kilowatt turbine; the SECAM colour television system, and extremely precise ballistic radar systems. The first French nuclear submarine was launched at Cherbourg in March 1967 but, unlike Britain, France did not have the benefit of American know-how.

The car industry is one of the most dynamic. France is the fifth biggest producer in the world and the second biggest exporter. 1966 was a record year in which output increased by twenty-three per cent, a rate unmatched in Europe or the United States. For the first time also the two-million mark was surpassed, the actual figure being 2,024,000 units. About 307,000 persons are employed in the car and bicycle industries. The biggest firm is the state-owned Renault, employing 63,000 and with a turnover in 1963 of $1.1 billion (£425 million). The other firms in order of size are Citröen, Peugeot and Simca which is associated with Rootes-Chrysler. Berliet now linked with Citröen is the principal builder of commercial vehicles. The car industry is largely concentrated in the Paris region, although all the firms now have large factories in the provinces.

One of the fastest-growing sectors of the economy is the chemical industry with an annual rate of expansion between 1949 and 1963 of 8.5 per cent and reaching 11.3 per cent in 1964. France is the fourth biggest exporter in the world after the United States, West Germany and Britain. About 365,000 persons are employed in the industry in which the leading firm is the Rhône-Poulenc complex concentrated in the Lyons area. Textiles is one of the country's traditional industries and has been given a boost by the development of man-made fibres. Today about half a million persons are employed in textiles, and Lyons, with its long tradition of silk weaving is again one of the main centres. Finally the building industry employs about 1.2 million persons excluding those working in electrical and steel construction firms. As in Britain, it is the chief source of employment for foreign workers. In 1965 the number of new dwellings completed was 410,000 in France compared to 391,000 in Britain.

Mention should be made of the aircraft industry which is engaged in the exciting co-operative venture with Britain of building the first supersonic airliner in the world, the Concord. The Sud-Aviation firm which is responsible for most of the airframe also designed the highly successful Caravelle in the 'fifties with the then startling innovation of having the jet engines at the rear.

FUEL AND POWER

At present France is obliged to import about half her requirements in fuel and power in spite of being well endowed with a diversity of sources of energy which include coal, natural gas, hydro-electric power and, until Algerian independence, oil. It is oil more than anything else which France lacks. In 1965 domestic output, principally from the Parentis oilfield in the Landes, was 2.9 million tons while consumption was 55.6 million tons. Under the fifth plan special efforts are being made to discover new oil wells in France, North Africa and the Middle East. France is fortunate that about forty per cent of her oil supply comes from the Algerian Sahara which is part of the franc zone, thus saving expenditure of precious foreign exchange. The refining industry is highly developed and in 1965 the sixteen refineries treated sixty-one million tons of crude oil.

COAL

Production, which is concentrated in the Nord and Pas de Calais departments and Lorraine, reached its peak in 1958 with sixty million tons, but since then output has been deliberately reduced by about a million tons a year and in 1965 came to fifty-four million tons. Thanks to the post-war modernisation efforts, the French coal mines have the reputation of being the most efficient in Europe. Britain, however, produces more than three times as much coal as France. The French Government has decided to make increasing use of American coal for the production of electricity and a growing proportion of the coalfields' output is being diversified in chemical by-products such as artificial fertiliser.

ELECTRICITY

Production, which has been rising steadily since the war, reached a record 109 thousand million kwh in 1966 and was about equally divided between thermal and hydro-electric sources. It is hoped that by 1970 nuclear energy plants will provide ten per cent of the required output but the French efforts in this field lag well behind those in Britain and towards the end of 1966 two of the Electricity Board's atomic reactors had to close down for more than six months following teething troubles. But it was at about the same time that General de Gaulle inaugurated the world's first tidal power generating plant on the Rance estuary in Brittany. When it is fully working it will produce 550 million kwh annually.

Although several more hydro-electric schemes remain to be built on the lower Rhône, future development will be concentrated on thermal centres whose unit costs are appreciably lower.

GAS

The gas industry, which was ninety-five per cent nationalised in 1946, received a tremendous boost from the discovery in 1951 of a rich source of natural gas at Lacq in the Pyrenees. The annual output from Lacq is the equivalent of over five million tons of coal and natural gas accounts for half the annual consumption, the rest being derived from coal and oil. Since 1951 the pattern of consumption has changed as gas becomes increasingly popular for domestic heating and cooking. Only a quarter of the annual production is now used for industrial purposes compared with forty-five per cent in 1951. It is interesting to note that the Lacq project also resulted in making France the fifth biggest producer of sulphur in the world with an annual output of 1.5 million tons or ten per cent of the world's production.

AGRICULTURE

The principal wealth of France has always been in the richness and diversity of her land and the increasing industrial development will hardly alter this basic fact in the foreseeable future. The explanation for the series of crises in the Common Market over the agricultural negotiations, especially the one in the summer of 1965, was principally French intransigence on what she regarded as her vital interests. How vital they are can be easily grasped from the following facts.

France's agricultural land, consisting of 342,300 square kilometres (136,000 square miles), accounts for almost half the useful arable land in the EEC and about a third of the Community's total production : forty per cent of the cereals, thirty-seven per cent of the meat, thirty-seven per cent of the milk and twenty-eight per cent of the cheese. At the 1962 census 3.8 million persons were working on the land or 20.7 per cent of the total active population, and the rural population as a whole was estimated at 8 million. (By 1965 the number working on the land had fallen to 18.2 per cent of the active population compared with only 3.5 per cent in Britain.) In 1964 the output from agriculture and forestry was estimated at 46,000 million francs ($9.2 billion, £3,300 million) or about nine per cent of total production. Industries transforming agricultural produce into food employed over half a million persons and turnover was about 40,000 million francs ($8 billion, £2,800 million). Agricultural produce and food account for one-sixth of French exports. Finally the maximum exploitation of the existing resources could support a population of a hundred million or twice the present one.

Pride is taken in the fact that productivity is increasing faster in agriculture than any other sector of the economy, having more than doubled between 1949 and 1961. The use of fertilisers has tripled since the war and the number of tractors has increased from 60,000 to almost a million. However, comparative statistics show that agricultural productivity over the past decade has risen faster in Britain and Spain than in France or the United States.

In France the exceptionally large number of small unprofitable farms, the result of the Napoleonic inheritance law enacting that estates be divided equally between children, hinders productivity. The Government has since 1949 concentrated on a policy of consolidation (*remembrement*) which is having impressive results extending annually to 1.4 million acres and reaching 1.8 million, it is hoped, by 1970. Between 1929 and 1963 the number of farms fell from 3.9 million to 1.9 million. In the same period the number of holdings of between 50 and 120 acres doubled and now account for a fifth of the total; a quarter are between twenty-five and fifty acres and another quarter between two and twelve acres. Only 1.3 per cent of holdings are over 250 acres.

The small family farm is the usual method of exploitation, covering fifty-five per cent of the cultivated land; a third is worked by tenant farmers and twelve per cent by share-croppers. Older farmers are being encouraged to hand over their holdings to a son or to leave the land altogether in return for a pension. Co-operative ventures are also being encouraged and expert advice on the latest techniques is available at over 800 study centres. The traditional suspicion of new-fangled methods, once so widespread among French farmers, is being rapidly replaced by an eagerness to profit from the new techniques.

Half the agricultural land is given over to the cultivation of cereals, especially wheat of which France is the fifth biggest producer in the world with an output of 13.8 million tons in 1964 (United States 35.1 million; Canada 16.3). The area under wheat has diminished considerably in France since the beginning of the century but the yield continues to rise, the average for the country being 31.5 quintals (just over three tons) per hectare (approximately two and a half acres) which is twice that of 1939. The fertile plains of northern France are the great wheat-growing areas. Barley and oats are also widely grown, although Britain produces more of the former crop than France, presumably to fulfil the demands of the brewing industry. Rice, introduced into France after the last war, is now grown extensively in the Rhône delta region and the supply is sufficient for home needs. Maize, which had previously been confined to the south-west, is now grown all over the country as a result of government incentives and production increased sevenfold between 1950 and 1960.

Vineyards cover one-fifteenth of the cultivated area and are found in most regions south of a line between Nantes and Reims. The cheaper table wines come from the Midi but until 1967, when the practice was forbidden, were usually blended with stronger Algerian wines to bring them up to the required strength. The choice wines whose quality is strictly controlled come from the Bordeaux region, Burgundy, the Loire valley, Alsace and the Champagne. Cognac or brandy is distilled from the vines grown in the Charente on the Atlantic coast. The annual wine output is about sixty million hectolitres (1,300 million gallons) and France and Italy are the leading wine producers in the world. Over-production has, however, frequently led to violent demonstrations by the wine-growers in the Midi protesting against falling prices and the importing of Algerian wine guaranteed under the Evian accord granting Algerian independence.

The principal wealth of French agriculture is in the herds of beef and dairy cattle which account for half the value of annual agricultural produce. The present livestock resources amount to 21 million cattle, 9 million pigs and 9 million sheep. France is the third biggest producer of cow's milk in the world with 20.4 million tons in 1964 or almost twice the British but only one-third of the U.S. output. Britain, however, produces

more than double the French amount of mutton and lamb. Beef-
steak is such a favourite French dish that in some years cattle
have to be imported, although France, with an output of 1.6
million tons of beef and veal in 1963, ranks as the fourth biggest
producer in the world. In the coming years the principal efforts
will be directed to increasing beef, fruit and vegetable production
with the Common Market farm fund theoretically assuring favourable prices and the disposal of surpluses without loss. In 1967
demonstrations in Brittany and Central France marked dissatis-
faction with the EEC prices on the part of small farmers.

FORESTS

Forests extend over 11.7 million hectares (28¼ million acres)
or twenty per cent of the national territory compared with 4¼
million acres in Britain and 520 million acres in U.S.A. About
forty-five per cent consists of full-grown timber and the rest is
coppice of which more than half is useful for commercial purposes.

FISHERIES

In 1964 there were 42,119 fishermen and 13,822 fishing
vessels. The catch (in 1,000 tons) was mainly fresh fish 398.6;
salted cod 50.8; crustaceans 19; shellfish 50.2 and oysters
62.1. The value of the total production was slightly over one
thousand million francs ($200 million, £72.3 million). The
British catch in the same year was valued at £60.3 million.

IMPORTS AND EXPORTS

A watershed year in the post-war evolution of France's external trade was 1958. Until that year there was a chronic
deficit from trade exchanges culminating in an adverse balance
in 1957 of more than 1,000 million dollars. The main reason
for this depressing pattern was the over-valuation of the franc,
and from the moment of its devaluation at the end of 1958,
reinforced by an austerity programme, a welcome surplus made
its appearance. The rate by which imports were covered by

exports rose from seventy-one per cent in 1957 to 103 per cent in 1961 (ninety-three per cent is reckoned as equilibrium under the French system of calculation). After a relapse into deficit in 1963 as a result of the rise in imports occasioned by the return of the Algerian settlers, the exchanges had again moved into surplus in 1965 although imports are tending to outstrip exports as the stabilisation plan introduced in 1963 is slowly relaxed.

The pattern of the trade exchanges in 1965 is shown by the following table:

	Exports per cent	Imports per cent
Manufactured goods	73.5	50.8
Food, drink, tobacco	15.9	17.3
Raw materials	7.4	16.4
Energy, oil	3.2	15.5

As the tariffs within the Common Market diminish, France is increasing trade with her five partners. Almost half of French exports went to EEC countries in 1965 compared with thirty-two per cent in 1950, and imports from that area increased during that period from twenty-three per cent to forty-five per cent. West Germany is France's biggest customer and supplier, accounting for almost a quarter of her exports and imports.

The pretty Normandy town of Honfleur, near the mouth of the Seine, was an important port in the sixteenth and seventeenth centuries. The early French colonisers of Canada and the West and East Indies set sail from here. In the nineteenth century Honfleur became a favourite haunt of artists of the Impressionist school, fascinated by the colours and light of the Normandy sky and landscape.

Great hopes for the economic future of Marseilles and the surrounding hinterland are pinned on the rapid development of the adjoining port of Fos. It already groups four oil refineries and dependent petro-chemical and chemical industries, and a steel manufacturing complex is being built. When the planned North Sea—Mediterranean waterway via the Rhône is completed, Marseilles and Fos will together form a 'Europort' capable, it is hoped, of rivalling Rotterdam.

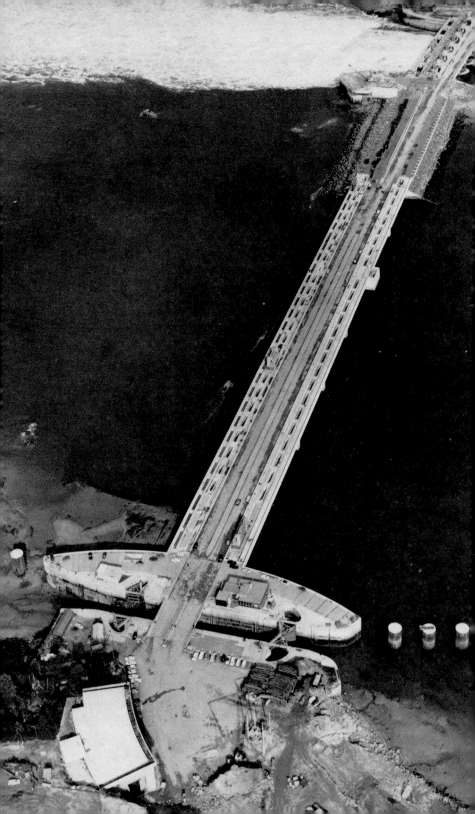

Outside the Common Market Britain is one of France's main trading partners and exchanges between them totalled $1 billion (£368 million) in 1965. The surplus in favour of France in 1958 had by 1963 changed to a $120 million (£43 million) deficit but in 1965 it had been reduced to about half. The following table compares the external trade of France with that of Britain and the United States in 1965 without including re-exports.

	Imports	Exports
	(thousand million dollars)	
France	10.34	10.05
Britain	15.69	13.21
USA	21.36	27.06 (foreign aid included)

The balance of payments in France has been consistently favourable between 1959 and 1966 thanks to tourist revenue and influx of long term capital. The surplus reached a record $1,147 million in 1961, but fell to about $340 million in 1966. As a result of this impressive performance over the period 1958-65, France was able to build up her reserves to over 5,000 million dollars and reduce her exterior debts from over

———

The world's first tidal power generating plant in the Rance estuary in Brittany. It was completed in 1966 at a cost of about $97 million (£36 million). From the left it consists of : a lock to allow shipping to pass up and down the river; the power station with twenty-four 'bulb' units which can serve as turbines or pumps; a fixed dyke; a moveable dam to help in filling and emptying the eight square miles of reservoir behind the barrage, and a dual-carriage road providing a new link between St Malo and Dinard. The total length of the barrage is 2,400 feet. Thanks to the exceptional rise and fall of the tides in the estuary, sometimes forty-four feet, and the dual role of the 'bulb' sets, output is 550 million kwh a year.

3,000 million dollars to 454 million dollars. But the halcyon days of a tourism surplus of ninety million dollars in 1963 had been replaced in 1965 by a small deficit, a result of the increasing number of French holidaymakers going abroad.

TRADE UNIONS

The French trade union movement is much less efficiently organised and less widely implanted than the British. Among the reasons given for the weakness of trade unionism in France are the reluctance of workers to contribute to union funds and the important place in the economy of the nationalised and semi-public sectors where special conditions prevail.

The law of 1791 forbidding all trade or professional groups was revoked in 1884 and since then trade unions or *syndicalisme* has been given a clear legal framework. No limit is put on the number of groups which may be formed and there is no obligation on anyone to join them. However, the larger ones which are recognised as being the most representative enjoy a special status when it comes to wage negotiations and labour relations.

The biggest grouping is the *Confédération Générale du Travail* with about 1.5 million members. The CGT is virtually controlled by the Communist party although not all the members are Communists. It is especially strong in the metallurgy, mining and printing industries. In 1947 the non-communist element in the CGT broke away, following the communist-inspired strikes that year, to form the *Confédération Générale du Travail-Force Ouvrière* which now has about 400,000 members. CGT-FO is influenced by the Socialist party but in no way remotely resembling the links between the British Labour party and the big unions. Most of its members are drawn from the public services. The third large trade union body is the *Confédération Française Démocratique du Travail* with 750,000 members. It disputes with the CGT the leadership in the mining and engineering industries and is particularly strong in the commercial sector. Originally inspired by specifically Catholic social principles, the CFDT dropped the word 'Christian' from its title in 1964 in an attempt to broaden its appeal. In recent years it has been even more militant than the CGT in calling for improved working conditions in the transport services. Finally the *Confédération Générale des Cadres* represents 150,000 technical staff and executives.

These confederations group the federations into which the various industries are organised. There are numerous other smaller unions which call themselves ' autonomous,' one of the most important being the teachers' federation. Theoretically the unions are non-political, but in practice, above all in the case of the CGT, political issues inevitably influence union policies.

The principal employers' organisation is the *Conseil National du Patronat Français* which in 1946 replaced the pre-war body dissolved for being tainted by collaboration with the Germans. The CNPF represents about a million firms and its role corresponds to that of the Confederation of British Industries with whom it has periodic consultations to examine the consequences of eventual British entry into the Common Market. Attached to the CNPF is the conservative-minded confederation of medium and small-sized businesses and the association of the younger and more dynamic owner-managers called *Centre National des Jeunes Patrons.*

LABOUR RELATIONS

French workers are protected by an impressive bulk of social legislation designed to ensure the fullest possible co-operation between management and labour and guarantee the rights of workers. The praiseworthy intentions of these laws have not prevented them from being difficult to work out in practice but they are being periodically amended to increase their effectiveness. The principal measures can be mentioned briefly.

Any firm which employs more than ten persons must have a number of ' delegates ' representing and elected by the employees to present their claims and complaints to the management which is obliged to receive them at least once a month and pay them for fifteen hours monthly devoted to staff affairs. Industrial firms with more than fifty employees and commercial firms with more than 500 must have a *comité d'entreprise* presided over by the owner or general manager and consisting of representatives elected by the employees for two years. The committee meets once a month and the members receive twenty hours' pay monthly for their time. The role of the committee is to run the various social amenities such as canteens and recreation facilities, but especially to ensure the association of the workers with the management of the firm; the latter is bound to consult the committee on technical, financial and commercial matters.

Much lip service is paid in France to the principle of associating the workers with the running of firms and giving them a share in profits derived from auto-investment. Thus the nationalised concerns can have representatives of the employees on the *conseil d'administration* which corresponds to the board in the British sense. Firms which have schemes for workers' participation in increased productivity or profit-sharing receive certain tax exonerations, but so far only 104,000 workers benefit from these contracts.

In the second half of 1967, General de Gaulle's long-cherished dream of ending the class war by associating workers with the fruits of enterprise was embodied in decrees introducing a controversial profit-sharing scheme. It applies to private firms with 100 or more workers and certain state-owned concerns while smaller firms may adopt it voluntarily.

Briefly the scheme consists of distributing on a fifty-fifty basis to a firm's employees and shareholders the profit which remains after tax, after paying a 'fair' return on capital employed, and after other complex adjustments. The amount due to the workers will be blocked for five years and will be distributed in one of three ways: (a) as shares in the company (b) as loans to the company by the workers who will receive bonds (c) as investments in unit trusts by the company. The scheme came into operation in 1969 when the 1968 trading results were known. About five million persons will be affected but the amounts distributed will be modest as, due to rather strange accounting methods, company profits in France tend to be meagre. It is estimated that one worker in five belongs to a firm which makes a loss.

A widespread practice is the collective agreements made between the employers of various industries and the trade unions, either on a national or regional level. The agreements normally cover minimum wages, retirement benefits, hours, holidays and so on, but if certain conditions are fulfilled the Government can compulsorily extend the agreement to cover all similar industries in a particular region after consultations with the employers and the most representative unions. Within certain industries such as cars and metallurgy, individual firms may draw up agreements on the lines of those common in the United States providing for supplementary benefits for the employees, periodic increases in wages geared to output and procedures to avoid strikes. Thus Renault has given the rest of the country the lead on the question of paid holidays; seventy per cent of workers have now four weeks annually following Renault's decision in 1962.

STRIKES

In recent years strikes, although fairly frequent, have tended in the nationalised sector to be limited to one or three days. Since 1963 strikes in national services such as transport, electricity and gas must be preceded by five days' notice. A feature of the periodic ' general strikes ' intended to paralyse transport and industry for twenty-four or forty-eight hours is their failure to get full support. This is due to lack of accord between the unions and because strike pay is either very meagre or non-existent. The general strike of May-June 1968, when about ten million workers were estimated to be on strike, was compared to the 1936 nation-wide strikes which resulted in the Popular Front Government granting unprecedented wage increases and improved conditions. The 1968 settlement gave a general 13 per cent wage increase, a package of improvements in working conditions and trade union rights, and a pledge of more participation by the workers in the running of businesses.

THE PROFESSIONS

A special respect in France is accorded to persons belonging to the liberal professions and their intelligence and training entitle them to be described as ' intellectuals ' in a general and not in a donnish sense. Some confusion may be caused for English-speaking persons by the fact that the French use the word *profession* to mean occupation, whether referring to a postman or an architect. Professional bodies are organised on similar lines to those in Britain and the United States, although qualifications are perhaps more strictly controlled by the State because of the extent to which all branches of education are subject to the central government administration.

The professions and the senior executive posts accounted for less than five per cent of the active population in the 1962 census and there were five men for every woman in this élite group.

OCCUPATIONS

The following table, based on figures in the official *Annuaire Statistique de la France* (1966), shows the structure of the working populations of France, Britain and the United States in 1964.

	France (1,000)	Britain (1,000)	USA (1,000)
Total population	48,416	54,213	192,120
Total active population	20,080	25,780	76,972
—men	13,629	16,987	51,118
—women	6,451	8,793	25,854
Agriculture, forests, fisheries	3,653	948	5,057
Mining and quarrying	294	660	578
Manufacturing industries	5,554	9,016	19,468
Building, public works	1,804	1,802	4,903
Gas, electricity, water	189	409	1,055
Commerce, banking, insurance	2,781	4,142	17,514
Transport and communications	1,130	1,736	3,756

Miscellaneous services	3,846	6,293	21,279
Armed forces	615	424	2,738
Unemployed	214	349	3,876

SALARIES AND WAGES

Almost everyone who has visited France wants to know how the French manage to live on what appear to be quite modest salaries. But the visitor tends to forget that the lowly-paid workers and petty functionaries who make up the bulk of the working population do not eat in the restaurants where tourists find themselves paying perhaps $15 (£5) for a meal for two persons. Nor does the average Parisian buy clothes in the chic boutiques for men and women in the fashionable quarters frequented by tourists.

However, even allowing for this, it must be admitted that there is a certain mystery surrounding the survival of the average wage earner in what is one of the dearest countries in Europe if not in the world.

The official statistics reveal that in 1964 the average annual salary was $2,200 (£790). In categories this ranged from $7,560 (£2,700) for the higher grade *cadres* (professions, senior executives) to $1,760 (£630) for manual workers. In between came the middle *cadres* ($3,720, £1,330) and *employés* ($1,930, £690). By 1968 these salaries had increased appreciably in terms of sterling, because of an annual increase of at least five per cent and the devaluation of the pound in 1967.

The average hourly rate for manual workers in 1964 was 70 cents (5s 2d), the best-paid being those in the printing industry ($1, 7s) and the worst paid the cleaners at 50 cents (4s). The basic working week is forty hours, but overtime is frequent in most industries, with time and a quarter paid up to forty-eight hours and time and a half beyond that. The average working week for all categories in 1965 was 45.6 hours.

PURCHASING POWER

In the last decade the cost of living rose faster in France than in the rest of the Common Market, Britain and the United States. If one hundred is taken as the index in 1958, by 1964 it was 130 in France compared to 115 in Britain and 107 in the United States. In France, however, wages have been rising even more sharply and if the cost of living doubled between 1949 and 1964 workers' wages quadrupled, so purchasing power could be said to have also doubled. The *cadres* have done even better, as their salaries have increased five-fold since 1949. However, it is estimated that hourly wage rates in France, when measured in terms of purchasing power, are only marginally higher than they were before the war and for Paris engineers they had only recovered their pre-war level in 1963. The explanation is the longer hours now worked by Frenchmen at higher rates and the improved social benefits and bonuses.

The least fortunate section of the working population is the estimated half-million called *smigards* from the initials of the ponderous title for the official guaranteed minimum wage. In June 1968 the rate was 60 cents (3s 9d) an hour in Paris. It is geared to the cost of living index, but recently the government has been slowly increasing the SMIG voluntarily. Agricultural workers have a slightly lower minimum wage.

Wage differentials between Paris and the provinces, which before the war ranged between twenty and fifty per cent, have now been brought down to about twenty-five per cent.

An enquiry made by the magazine *Paris-Match* into the purchasing power of workers in France and the United States showed that in March 1967 the average hourly wage for a French worker was 3.70 francs compared with 13.90 francs for his American counterpart. Taking the weekly wage of a Paris metal worker as 202.5 francs ($40, £15 15s) the article drew the following conclusions: the American worker earns the price of a Chevrolet in thirteen weeks; the French worker earns his $1,200 (£450) Renault in twenty-six weeks. For a refrigerator the comparison is 63 hours and 291 hours; for a good pair of shoes, three hours and ten hours; for a chicken twenty-seven minutes and one hundred minutes.

WOMEN AT WORK

One-third of the French working population are women and contrary to popular belief there are proportionately less women working today than sixty years ago. Their role continues to grow in importance as they accede to more qualified posts. The 6.5 million women working are distributed in roughly equal proportions between agriculture, factories, routine clerical jobs and services and, finally, highly-qualified posts. They are in the majority in teaching and textiles and equal with men in banks, insurance and commerce generally.

The pattern of female employment has changed drastically since the beginning of the century. While the numbers fell in agriculture (by two million), textiles, domestic services and the garment industry, they rose significantly in gas, electricity, oil, chemicals, metallurgy and especially commerce and banking. What has been described as 'an astounding revolution' took place between the census years of 1954 and 1962 when the numbers of women in the liberal professions (especially teaching) and higher executive posts rose by sixty-six per cent, which was double the rate for men.

France was one of the first countries to sign the international convention urging equal pay for men and women for similar work and claims today that her record in this field (ten per cent gap) is one of the best in Europe. At a recent trade union assembly it was claimed, however, that the gap in some industries such as metallurgy was as high as twenty-two per cent.

It would be an unforgivable omission in a section on 'Women at Work' to ignore the enormous amount of unpaid work which is done in the home. Two French economists have estimated that a housewife with three children puts in a working week of seventy-seven hours. Another study made on the 'useful employment of time' divided up the annual total for France of 105,000 million hours as follows (figures in thousand millions): transport to and from work—five; studies—twelve; paid work—forty-three; unpaid household work—forty-five.

It is interesting to note that until 1938 in France married women were legally *incapable*, that is they had no separate existence in the eyes of the law. This inferiority dated back to 1804 when Napoleon, inspired by the Roman practice, insisted on the husband being endowed literally with the 'lord and master' role in the household. In practice many of the legal restrictions on women were ignored, but it was not until 1965 that a married woman became empowered to open a bank account without her husband's permission and to dispose of her personal property with complete freedom. How far the law has been removed from reality for the past 150 years is shown by the well-established fact that in the vast majority of French homes the wife controls the family budget and even gives the husband pocket money. One sociologist's definition of a *ménage* or household is that a man hands over his entire pay packet to a woman.

UNEMPLOYMENT

Unemployment in post-war France has never attained serious proportions. In 1967 alarm was expressed when the rate reached 370,000 or just under 2 per cent of the total labour force, compared to 2.4 per cent in Britain, 6.3 per cent in Italy, and 5 per cent in the United States. The rise in unemployment in the second half of the sixties was due principally to the slow-down in the economy provoked by the 1963 stabilisation plan and by the arrival on the labour market of the young people born in the high birth-rate years in the late forties.

Relatively few unemployed were on the dole (31,000 in 1965) until the new measures introduced in 1967 to cope with the new situation. Unemployment assistance is not part of the social security system and until 1967 was administered by a limited number of local unemployment funds, so that only persons living in districts where there were such funds could benefit from them. The daily rate in 1968 in the Paris region was $1.20 (10s 6d) for the head of the family and 48 cents (4s 1d) for the spouse or a dependent person. Compensation is also paid for temporary reductions in the working week and 70,000 persons received these benefits in 1965, mostly in the textile, garment and metal industries. A complementary system of unemployment insurance operates in the industrial and commercial trades covering about eight million workers. The benefits amount to thirty-five per cent of wages for the first nine months of unemployment.

Under the new measures a national labour exchange was set up to increase the mobility of labour and the dole was increased slightly and extended to the whole country. The complementary scheme was also extended to most workers, so that an unemployed person who had been earning $140 (£58) a month would receive eighty per cent of his pay during the early months of unemployment.

SICKNESS AND INJURY BENEFITS

These come under the social security system. A worker on sick leave receives the equivalent of half-pay. Invalids' benefits vary according to the degree of incapacity and vary from thirty to fifty per cent of the average salary for the last ten years. Compensation for accidents at work normally covers the full cost of medical and surgical expenses, functional readaptation and professional re-education. In the case of permanent incapacity the victim receives a pension which amounts to his basic salary if he is one hundred per cent incapacitated. If the accident or occupational illness is fatal the dependants are eligible for the pension.

Hygiene and security committees are obligatory in large enterprises, and since 1946 periodic inspections have been carried out by a corps of industrial health specialists, but twenty years later their number is still regarded as inadequate.

IMMIGRATION

Emigration is virtually non-existent in France. On the contrary, since the beginning of the century there has been constant recourse to immigrant labour to swell out the static or diminishing domestic labour force. Of the 1.8 million foreigners in

France, Algerians excepted, the Italians (645,000) are the most numerous, followed by the Spaniards and the Poles. Since the war the pattern of immigration has changed. The Spaniards have been the most numerous of the new arrivals, reaching a peak of 66,000 in 1964. The following year the number had fallen to 50,000 and seemed likely to be overtaken by the Portuguese, whose annual entry rate had climbed from 1,000 in 1955 to 47,000 in 1965. For seasonal immigration the Spaniards are easily the most numerous, totalling 87,000 in 1963. Most of the foreign workers are directed to the building industry. A total of 151,000 immigrants were placed in jobs by the National Immigration Office in 1965.

The influx of Algerian workers varies widely from year to year, and if arrivals outnumbered departures by 43,000 in 1963 a balance amounting to 11,000 in the other direction appeared in 1965. Since the war the labour force has been increased by a quarter of a million Algerian workers.

5

How They Learn

The French pride in their educational system, which they regard as the best in Europe if not in the world, does not prevent them from continuously criticising it. Since the war the traditional system has been subjected to a series of sweeping reforms and upheavals which reached a peak under the Fifth Republic. But in spite of all the changes, the administrative strait-jacket which Napoleon and other nineteenth-century reformers devised remained until the student upheaval in May 1968 forced the Government to liberalise the university system.

State education in France until 1968 consisted of a giant pyramid called the *Université de France,* at the apex of which stood the Minister of Education and which widened out to take in the universities, advanced institutes, secondary schools, technical schools, primary schools and infant classes. This immense and rigid hierarchic structure with its twelve million pupils—almost a quarter of the population—was ruled from an old mansion in a quiet Paris street called the Rue de Grenelle. The role of the local authorities, so important in Britain and the United States, is limited in France to contributing to the cost of school buildings and their upkeep. Virtually all the teachers, from primary to secondary level, are civil servants under the minister's direct control. The degree of centralisation was so great that the story is

often told about the minister who announced to Napoleon III :
' At this moment, in all the lycées in France, all the pupils are
construing a Latin text.' Teachers nowadays, needless to say,
have somewhat more freedom.

On the local level France was divided into twenty-three regions
called *académies*. At the head of each academy was a rector who
represented the minister and was responsible for all branches of
education in the region, from the university down to the infant
school. Under the rector, non-university education in each
department was controlled by academic inspectors who were
assisted by various councils and staffs of school inspectors.

Parallel to the system of public education, which is free and
secular, is the network of private, fee-paying schools called the
enseignement libre, most of which are run by Catholic religious
orders. In 1966-7 almost two million pupils, or one-sixth of the
total, were attending these schools. The idea of State subsidies
being paid to private schools is still anathema to many left-
wing politicians, and it is only since 1959 that a system of direct
aid for these schools has been in operation. About 12,000 private
schools have signed contracts with the State, which pays the
teachers' salaries in return for the right to inspect them and the
obligation to recruit properly-qualified staff. The curriculums
and teaching methods follow closely those in State schools, as
only public examinations are recognised.

The public education system evolved slowly throughout the
nineteenth century. Napoleon laid down the lines for university
and secondary instruction, but free compulsory primary education was not introduced until 1884 by the great reformer Jules
Ferry. The drawback of the highly centralised system was that
the different orders—primary, secondary and higher—tended
to form enclosed universes and perpetuate social divisions, as the
children of poorer parents received little encouragement to pass
from the primary school to the secondary *lycée* where the
emphasis on classical subjects was geared to university requirements. At university level there grew up another type of segrega-
tion which remains today, namely between the university proper
and the *grandes écoles* or advanced engineering colleges, the

most famous of which is the *Ecole Polytechnique*. Napoleon's idea was that the university faculties would train teachers, lawyers and doctors, while the *grandes écoles* trained the technicians and administrators. Yet a further division in the educational system appeared in the present century with the growth of technical schools which were grafted on to the secondary system.

The barriers between primary and secondary education became even more formidable in the pre-war period when the school-leaving age was raised from twelve to fourteen in 1936, but the new classes formed to provide post-primary education remained attached to the primary schools. The *écoles normales* in each department for training primary teachers were filled from the primary schools. At the same time the prestigious *lycées* began to extend downwards and form special preparatory classes attached to them. The result of this segregationist policy was that in 1939 only one university student in forty was the son of a manual worker, while one in four was the son of a civil servant.

In October 1968, a Higher Education Reform Bill made the universities autonomous in administration, teaching and finance. Elected councils of teaching staff and students replaced the once all-powerful rectors in the running of the universities, and freedom of political debate is allowed subject to certain conditions. The old faculties were abolished and replaced by more independent 'teaching and research units.'

The *démocratisation* of education has been hindered, however, by the effects of the demographic revolution mentioned in chapter one which meant that, since 1950, a wave of 200,000 children arrives each year at the age for compulsory schooling (six years old). Impressive efforts have been made to accelerate the school building programme and provide the necessary teachers. The education budget for 1965, at 15,000 million francs ($3 billion, £1,100 million) was almost five times greater than in 1952; about the same percentage of national expenditure as in Britain. Under the fifth plan it was hoped, between 1966 and 1970, to create 7,600 infant classes; 19,200 primary classes;

over one million places in secondary schools; and by 1972 to have increased university accommodation to 793,000 students compared with 327,000 in 1964 (American universities for 1966 totalled 6.4 million students).

SCHOOLING

School begins for most French children in urban areas at the end of their second year, when they enter the *école maternelle* or nursery school for three years' non-compulsory pre-primary school education. At the end of their fifth year compulsory education begins in primary schools, and ends five years later when the secondary stage is reached. Children entering the ' first cycle ' (eleven to fifteen years) are, at an early stage, divided according to aptitude into those who will probably continue secondary schooling to the end of the ' second cycle ' (fifteen to eighteen) and those who will receive a ' terminal ' education and leave at the end of the compulsory period. At the end of the second cycle the students sit for the *baccalauréat* examination. This gives admittance to universities, but not to the *grandes écoles*, which have their own special entrance examinations and demand several years' extra study. That is the

———

The Escale Dam on the Durance, the Alpine river which has been tamed by Electricité de France to generate 6,000 million kwh annually. The waters of the river have also been canalised to allow the irrigation of about 200,000 acres of agricultural land in the lower Rhône valley, producing melons, tomatoes and early vegetables.

system in its barest outline. Clearly it approximates to those used in Britain and the United States, but when it is examined in more detail important distinguishing features emerge.

Infant School

Over two million children between two and six at present attend 6,400 nursery schools or infant classes attached to primary schools. Some 25,000 female teachers, called *institutrices*, teach their young charges physical exercises with emphasis on proper breathing and agility, and much of the time is devoted to games, painting and decoration. But particular attention is paid to correct speech, and the brighter children are encouraged to read. Methods are frequently based on the Montessori and other original techniques.

Primary School

There are three courses, ' preparatory ' (six to seven), ' elementary ' (seven to nine) and ' intermediary ' (nine to eleven). If the pupils are numerous enough the classes are distinct, but

———

Medical students following a lecture in a modern amphitheatre in Strasbourg University. The vacant places are in contrast with the serious overcrowding in the Paris faculties, which attract a disproportionate number of students from the provinces.

The new science faculty of Paris University follows tradition by being on the left bank of the Seine. It is already full to capacity and another faculty has been built in the suburbs.

often in village schools they are all grouped together, with forty regarded as the desirable maximum. In small schools boys and girls are together; in the larger ones they are usually separated. Retarded or physically handicapped children are cared for in special institutes.

Class usually begins at 8.30 am and goes on until 11.30, when there is a two-hour break for lunch which may be taken in the school canteen for about 50 cents (4s). Children of poor parents pay less or nothing at all. Instruction and books are free for all. Class resumes at 1.30 pm and ends three hours later. These hours may be varied somewhat, especially for the younger children, but the average, including recreations and physical education, is thirty hours a week. The main emphasis is on writing and speaking French correctly and on arithmetic. Other subjects are history and geography, practical science including drawing, citizenship and one hour of music lessons, which may be singing. There is a full day's class every day except Thursday and, of course, Sunday. Since no religious instruction is given in the State schools, parents are encouraged to provide this on Thursdays if they wish. No homework is given; but parents are informed monthly of their children's progress and are periodically shown their corrected exercises.

Corporal punishment is forbidden in schools; the punishments given for poor work range from a bad mark to detention or exclusion from a class.

There are at present 72,000 primary schools in which 5.5 million children are taught by more than 200,000 teachers (*instituteurs*). There are 10,000 private schools with 800,000 pupils.

Secondary School

Before the present reforms, entrance into secondary schools was based on a competitive examination somewhat like the eleven-plus. The brighter pupils then entered the ' sixth class ' (classes are numbered from sixth to first in ascending order) in a *lycée* which was the equivalent of an American high school, and

spent seven years preparing for the *baccalauréat*, called familiarly *bac* or *bachot,* a very stiff examination in two parts corresponding to a high school or private secondary school diploma.
The children who failed the entrance examination were diverted
to post-primary classes in which they were given a rudimentary
technical or commercial training until school-leaving age, when
they were awarded a *Certificat d'Etudes Primaires* if successful
in a final test. These classes were given in a *Collège d'Enseignement Général* or general education college provided by the local
authorities and corresponding to the secondary modern school in
Britain.

The competitive entrance examination into secondary schools
has now been abolished, but children passing from a private
school to a State secondary school must sit for a qualifying examination. Instead, all children enter the first cycle (eleven to
fifteen), but a special commission decides at this stage, after
examining the children's progress over the past few years, if they
have the ability to follow a course of theoretical studies. If so,
they enter a ' general section ' and after the first three months
the teacher advises the parents whether their child should follow
a classical or modern course. If not, the less endowed child
enters ' transition classes ' lasting two years, followed by a
further two years of practical training which may be agricultural,
artisanal, commercial or industrial and which will be specified
on the *Diplôme de Fin d'Etudes.*

The essential element about this observation or guidance stage
is that all the courses should be followed in the same school so
that a child in the transition classes who later showed special
talents could transfer to a classical or modern course. At the
end of the second year in secondary school (fifth class), a second
orientation decides which of five courses, two classical, two
modern and one practical, all crowned by *baccalauréats*, a
pupil will follow. Yet a third *orientation* is made two years later
at the end of the first cycle, at the age of fifteen, when it is
decided whether the pupil will follow a long or short course.
The long course will continue in a *lycée* for another three years
(second, first and terminal class) to the *baccalauréat,* while the

short course, lasting one or two years, will give a specialised practical training in a technical *lycée* or technical college, at the end of which an appropriate *brevet* or certificate will be awarded. Pupils who originally went into transition classes intending to leave school as soon as possible can later decide to take one of the 'short courses.'

At present this complicated series of reforms is at a half-way stage with elements of the new system coexisting with the remnants of the old, much to the confusion of parents, teachers and, of course, the children themselves. One of the most interesting developments is perhaps the steadily increasing number of *Collèges d'Enseignement Secondaire,* the equivalent of the British comprehensive school or the American high school where all three streams, long, short and transition, are 'under the same roof' until the end of the first cycle at the age of fifteen.

The *baccalauréat* is no longer in two parts, but students who fail at the first attempt in June are allowed a second attempt in September if they reach a certain average. Special refresher courses are televised during August. There are now five kinds of *baccalauréat* which permit entrance to a corresponding university faculty, and two diplomas as industrial or commercial technician which will give entrance to the new *Instituts Universitaires de Technologie* (IUT), rather like the colleges of advanced technology in Britain. Bac A is a classical and literary examination of six or seven subjects, including philosophy. Bac B specialises in economics and social science. Bac C and Bac D consist of seven subjects, but concentrate on mathematics and science, although philosophy and a modern language are obligatory. Bac E or *Bac Technique* is similar to D, but the course includes twelve hours extra a week of technology and workshop instruction. This course, which is regarded as very difficult, has not so far attracted the numbers required to fulfil the fast-growing demand for engineers.

All the ambitious plans for the reshaping of secondary education to cater for the country's growing need for engineers and technicians are being jeopardised by the scarcity of science and mathematics teachers; but this is a problem which most industrialised countries are facing today.

Higher Education

University education is free, except for low entrance and examination fees. Under the 1968 reform, the twenty-three former academies are being progressively replaced by about fifty universities, each consisting of between 6,000 and 18,000 students. The former faculties have been replaced by the modern-sounding 'teaching and research units' which will number about 600 when the adaptation process is completed during the 1970s. The key words in the wide-ranging reforms are autonomy and participation. Thus each unit elects its own governing body from teachers and students, and has considerable freedom to decide its own statutes. Another key factor in the reform is the emphasis on 'interdisciplinary' cooperation. Under the old system the one hundred schools of law, medicine, science, letters and pharmacy were rigidly distinct and often situated in different towns in the case of the one university. Now the new universities are obliged to associate arts, letters and the sciences as much as possible. The reforms are being carried out gradually and not without disturbances, notably in Paris where the once sprawling university of over 100,000 students is being broken up into smaller units. As well as the state universities, there are several Catholic colleges called *instituts*, attended by about 20,000 students. The students must sit for the state examinations, however, to obtain a degree.

University courses follow a similar pattern to those in Britain and the United States. A *licence*, corresponding to a bachelor's degree, is awarded at the end of a three-year successful course in letters and science and after four years in law and economic science. A simple diploma is awarded after two years. An extra year's study can lead to a master's degree in letters and science. Doctorates take at least six years, more often ten in arts for the preparation of the two dissertations required.

An astonishing amount of higher education is carried on outside the universities altogether in the famous *grandes écoles* or great schools, which may have no connection with the Ministry of Education. Most of them train engineers, the best-known being the *Ecole Polytechnique* in Paris, under the Ministry of the Armed Forces, and the schools for mining and highway engineers. *Lycée* professors and future administrators study in the *Ecole Normale Supérieure,* also in Paris, and the latter, as we have seen in Chapter Two are also trained in the *Ecole Nationale d'Administration.* Other advanced schools are those for oriental languages, political studies and the *Ecole des Chartes* for librarians and archivists. The oldest is the *Collège de France* founded in 1529 in Paris. It specialises in literature and science.

The entrance examinations for the *Ecole Normale* and the *Polytechnique* are highly competitive and nine out of ten fail. To prepare for them, the most brilliant school-leavers stay on for two years after the *baccalauréat* to study in special classes in the best Paris *lycées.* The graduates of these two higher schools are the nearest French equivalent to the Eton-Harrow-Oxford-Cambridge old boy network. *Polytechniciens* are known mysteriously as *les X,* and a large number of the top administrative posts in the nationalised enterprises and industry are filled by them. The *normaliens,* renowned for their practical jokes, enjoy an even higher intellectual prestige if they do not end up making quite as much money. The President, M Pompidou, is a *normalien,* as are several other members of the Government. M Pompidou, incidentally, was first a professor in a Paris *lycée* before becoming an administrator in Rothschilds Bank and finally Prime Minister before even being elected to Parliament.

Most of the 112 engineering colleges throughout the country are of university standard even if they do not rank as *grandes écoles.* Architects are trained in the *Ecole des Beaux Arts,* which is controlled by the Ministry for Cultural Affairs.

Although higher education is virtually free, many students need financial help for equipment and lodgings. The distribution and amount of *bourses* is regulated by two specialised bodies, one for secondary schools and the other for universities. At present there are over a million secondary school students receiving aid which varies according to their parents' circumstances, and about 100,000 university students. In addition, students in certain higher institutes who guarantee to enter public service for a certain period are paid by the ministry concerned, as are trainee teachers.

The numbers attending French universities have increased at a staggering rate: 80,000 in 1939, 125,000 in 1949, 511,000 in 1967. This last figure is over twice that for Britain, and by 1970 is expected to be 550,000. About forty-three per cent are women, compared to twenty-eight per cent in Britain in 1959. It is difficult to compare the number of school-leavers in each country who go on to university, as military service sometimes causes a postponement of university studies in France. The fifth plan forecasts the following pattern for 1975: for every 100 pupils finishing the first cycle of secondary education at the age of sixteen, twenty will begin working, forty-five will enter the short second cycle for technical training and thirty-five the long cycle; of this last figure, fifteen will start working immediately after school, eight will enter the university institutes of technology and twelve the university faculties. Statistics of the Ministry of Education for 1964-5 showed that, of the total population aged between nineteen and twenty-two, almost seven per cent were at a university. If the engineering colleges and *grandes écoles* are taken into account the percentage of the student-age population receiving higher education is estimated at fifteen per cent, compared to forty per cent in the United States and ten per cent in Britain.

The Ministry of Education publishes a table showing the social origins of French university students. Some of the categories into which the parents' occupations are divided have no exact equivalent in Britain or the United States.

Social origins of university students—June 1965

	per cent
Farmers	5.5
Farm labourers	.7

Employers   15.2
Professions, administrators   30.2
Middle-grade executives and primary
    school teachers   17.7
Employees   8.2
Manual workers   8.3
Domestic personnel   1.2
Rentiers   6.0
Others, including policemen   6.5
Indeterminate   .5

In a debate in the National Assembly in June 1967, the Minister of Education, M Peyrefitte, interpreted these figures as proving that sixty per cent of university students came from non-privileged families. Nevertheless, French universities do not seem to have been opened up to the working classes to the same extent as in Britain where, according to the Robbins Report, a quarter of undergraduates come from the homes of manual workers.

MAIN DIFFERENCES

French parents, like those in any other country, are extremely anxious that their children should successfully complete their secondary schooling and thus have the opportunity to benefit from a higher education, but the *baccalauréat* is such a difficult examination that school life is geared exclusively to getting good results. Sports are indeed compulsory and physical tests are part of the *bac* but the time which can be given to them is limited compared with British schools. Playing fields are scarce and inter-school competitions rare. In spite of the long hours of study and the urging of parents and teachers, the failure rate in the *bac* tends to be high, especially in mathematics, in which only forty-five per cent were successful in 1966. The strain on the final year students is great, and can be seen in the explosion of emotions which accompanies the *monôme* or rag day in Paris when the *bac* is over. In 1966 the *monôme* consisted of a day of running fights between the police and the students, who let off steam by wrecking cafés and blocking traffic, so it was banned the following year.

Boarding schools, known as *internats*, are not numerous, as the State system of education consists mainly of day schools. Consequently there is no real equivalent of the British public school with its emphasis on character-building and games. The private schools, run by nuns and priests for the most part, are small, and in Paris a certain snob value is attached to them. The nearest things to the best British public schools or U.S. exclusive private schools are a few *lycées* in Paris such as *Louis-le-Grand,* where the best pupils prepare for the *grandes écoles.*

The school year is not long compared with other European countries. It begins about the middle of September for the primary schools, a week later for the secondary. The Christmas holiday is limited to ten days and there is a four-day mid-term break in February. The Easter holidays last a fortnight and primary and secondary schools break up finally at the end of June.

Life in the universities varies according to their size, which ranges from Paris with 100,000 students to Reims with 2,000. The faculties are usually not residential as in the U.S.A., and the students who do not live at home board, if they are lucky, in hostels or a *cité universitaire* on the lines of an American campus (ten per cent). Forty-five per cent live in lodgings and forty per cent at home. Undergraduates frequently complain that the discipline in the student residences is too strict, being modelled on that in the *lycées,* where military uniforms were worn up to the end of the last century. Visiting between the male and female quarters is strictly controlled; several years ago hundreds of police were called in to break up students demonstrating at the Antony residence outside Paris against the construction of a porter's lodge at the entrance to the women's quarters.

The number of Paris students, ten times that of Oxford or Cambridge, means that student facilities are frequently inadequate. Library space is so difficult to find that many students

have to study in cafés, depending on the tolerance of waiters.
Lecture halls are so crowded that students sit on the professor's
rostrum. Their rooms are often garrets in old buildings in the
Latin Quarter, without heating or running water. It may be
necessary to travel miles for lectures; the faculty of letters is now
scattered between the Sorbonne proper, the *Grand Palais* on the
Champs Elysées and the suburb of Nanterre. The failure rate in
France is high, and it is estimated that only one university
student in five graduates, compared to two in five in Britain.
However, the wastage is not as great as it might seem, since
many students enrol in universities with the intention of obtaining only certain certificates of the four or five which make up
the bachelor's degree. Also, more French students take part-time
jobs during term than in Britain, with a consequent adverse effect
on their studies.

INDUSTRIAL AND PROFESSIONAL TRAINING

As already remarked, after leaving school this type of training
is given mainly in institutes distinct from university faculties. The
best-known are the *Conservatoire des Arts et Métiers*, the *Ecole
Centrale des Arts et Manufactures*, the *Ecole des Hautes Etudes
Commerciales* of the Paris Chamber of Commerce and the
National Agronomic Institute, all in Paris. In the provinces there
are numerous schools of engineering, agriculture, forestry and
fine arts.

Adult education courses have been given extensive government
encouragement since 1959 when a policy of *promotion sociale*
was started to try and ' recuperate ' gifted young persons who had
gone to work instead of university. In 1964, $50 million (£18
million) was allotted by the Government to these largely technical
and engineering courses, which were followed by 440,000 persons, mainly in night classes. The success of this scheme is
threatened by a grave shortage of qualified teachers. The
National Pedagogic Institute in Paris runs an extensive service
of correspondence courses complemented by classes on radio
and television. As well as benefiting children unable to attend

school because of illness, the courses are also designed for adult workers and future teachers. In 1965 the number of the Institute's pupils was 110,000 and was increasing by 20,000 annually.

6

How They Get About

GETTING about is no trouble to the French, who have one of the best rail systems in the world, are preceded by only the Americans, Canadians and Swedes as the most highly motorised people, and dispose of a network of roads which have been the envy of Europe since the Roman occupation. For travelling abroad there is *Air France* which proudly claims the most extensive range of services in the world and for more luxurious trips the *France*, one of the fastest and best equipped liners afloat, is available. There is, however, another side to the picture : the accident toll on French roads is appalling. Paris and other cities are engaged in a race against time to stave off imminent traffic paralysis with a crash programme of clearways and underground car parks; the lack of sufficient motorways or *autoroutes* can make long-distance car trips in holiday periods a nightmare; and in another element the merchant fleet is struggling for survival against more powerful rivals.

Transport is, of course, one of the most important sectors in the economy and in 1965 the total number of persons employed in the various services was 816,000 or almost five per cent of the active population.

RAILWAYS

The French railway network is the third largest in the world after the United States and the Soviet Union. There were 23,000 miles of track in operation in 1965 compared with 15,000 miles in Britain. About 2,500 miles of track were closed down over the past decade for economic reasons and there will be further closures in the less populated regions of about one-third of the present system. The man whose name is most closely associated with French railways is the world-wide known engineer, Louis Armand, who in the post-war period was responsible for the rapid and successful recovery and modernisation programme.

The nationalisation of the railways dates from 1938 when the *Societé Nationale des Chemin de Fer* (SNCF) was set up with the State holding a fifty-one per cent interest and the rest of the capital divided among the former operators. The administrative board consists of eighteen members—ten State representatives, three representing the private shareholders and five the personnel. The SNCF is easily the biggest enterprise in France with 360,000 employees and an annual turnover of about $2.2 billion (£920 million). Before the war there were 200,000 more on the payroll, so productivity per head has increased by sixteen per cent.

This progress has been overshadowed by that achieved by locomotive power, where the replacement of steam by electricity and diesel power has increased productivity by 360 per cent and has led to a relative decrease in energy consumption of seventy per cent. The electrification programme is now in its final stages and at present seventy per cent of rail traffic is on the electrified system. Steam locomotives, which now account for less than a quarter of the total traffic, are being rapidly replaced by diesel trains. The electrified lines are, for the most part, those linking Paris to the principal provincial capitals, and they totalled over 5,000 miles in 1965. The Paris-Toulouse express, called the *Capitole*, is claimed to be the fastest train in Europe. It now does the 420-mile journey in six hours, using the new French designed BB-9200 electric locomotive which reaches a speed of 125 mph on some stretches.

Like British Rail, however, the SNCF finds it impossible to break even, and the deficit in 1966 was estimated at £83 million. An important factor in the deficit is the increasing competition from private road haulage firms for the transport of merchandise and the enormous increase in the number of cars (multiplied by five between 1951 and 1964), which has slowed down the growth of passenger traffic (100 million in 1964). In the past five years the pattern of merchandise traffic has altered little, with rail, road and waterways sharing it in the percentages of sixty-three, twenty-seven and ten per cent respectively. According to the fifth plan, the railway's share should fall to fifty-five per cent by 1970, but to the benefit of pipelines transporting petroleum products rather than road haulage.

During the seventies France will pioneer what promises to be the most exciting development in rail traffic, namely the *aérotrain* or hovertrain, which embodies the principle of the British invention known as the hovercraft. The hovertrain has been developed by the French engineer, M Bertin. It runs on a special track which is an inverted T-beam of prestressed concrete with an eighteen-inch high vertical flange of concrete or metal over which the train squats, with air blowers providing friction-less supports. Early in 1967, after extensive tests on a half-scale model, the Government decided to build the first line between Paris and Orléans, seventy-five miles away. The first stage will consist of a twelve mile stretch outside Orléans, costing over $7 million (£3 million), which will be used to determine construction costs, the cost per passenger mile and the safe maximum speed. The designers claim that the train can travel safely at 250 mph. The Government's long-term plans foresee a network of hovertrain services linking major cities and also linking Paris to its future satellite towns. Several American companies are interested in the French system and a first line between New York and Montreal is being studied.

By 1975 it was hoped that the British and French rail systems would be directly linked by means of the long-awaited Channel Tunnel. Both countries have now decided that on account of its length the tunnel should be for rail traffic only and that the

French and British rail companies would be closely associated with the public operating body. The cost is estimated at $408 million (£170 million) at 1966 prices. The work had not started by mid-1970.

ROADS

Successive French rulers made a point of improving on the impressive legacy of national highways which the Romans left behind. There was a strategic reason for this concentration on road building, as Paris was always uneasily conscious of the need to be able to rush troops to trouble-spots in the provinces. By the end of the seventeenth century the medieval cart tracks which served for roads began to be replaced by the long, straight, paved routes which Colbert, Louis XIV's finance minister, constructed to speed up the postal services. Napoleon, ever conscious of military requirements and the need to strengthen the centralising influence of Paris, carried on the task. In the northern half of France the flat, undulating nature of the terrain allowed the engineers to run their roads like rulers, dead straight as far as the eye could see. The geometrical effect was increased by the regular grassy margins and the rows of trees, usually poplars or planes, like sentinels on each side.

Alongside the trunk road system, called *routes nationales*, a more extensive network of *routes départementales* was developed and completed by *chemins vicinaux* or by-roads, maintained by the local *communes*. In 1964 the road system measured 485,000 miles, of which 50,000 miles were trunk roads and 173,000 miles departmental roads. As a rule both types of road are kept in good condition, although flooding and frost frequently do serious damage to those traversing the mountainous regions, especially the Alps. The departmental roads, which are usually omitted from touring maps, often provide excellent ways of escaping from the strain of driving on the main roads with their increasingly heavy truck traffic. Yet French motorists continue to shun them in spite of the urging of motoring associations to avoid the principal routes on holiday weekends.

It is not surprising that the traditional road system has proved inadequate at holiday times, given the tremendous increase in the number of cars over the past fifteen years, from 1.7 million in 1951 to over nine million today. The ever-mounting accident toll reflects this car boom : 4,000 persons were killed on French roads in 1952 and 12,277 in 1966, while injuries soared from 80,000 to 292,000. Increased police surveillance seems to have little effect in reducing the accident toll. Almost in desperation, the Government, in the summer of 1966, instructed prefects all over the country to enforce their powers to withdraw on the spot the licences of motorists caught driving in a dangerous manner. To help track down the offenders, traffic police disguised themselves as ordinary citizens out for a drive with their wives and families. When these ' Q-cars ' spotted a flagrant traffic offence such as overtaking dangerously or crossing the continuous yellow line, they radioed the offender's number to a motorcycle patrol waiting further on. The startled offender soon found himself in front of a roadside court in the open air consisting of the prefect, a police officer and a representative of a motoring organisation. In most cases the offender's licence was withdrawn for a temporary period and he was asked to appear before a permanent tribunal at a later date. At the end of the year the Minister of

The University of Caen was founded in 1432 but the new buildings (opposite) date from 1958. The bronze phoenix in the foreground symbolises the renaissance of the university which is attended by over 8,000 students.

the Interior claimed that the accident statistics showed that there
had been a significant decrease in road deaths during the period
of 'instant justice.' Following protests from the motoring or-
ganisations, the practice of making the offending driver abandon
his car and walk to the nearest garage was dropped, however.
Doubts continue to be expressed by jurists on the legality of the
roadside courts.

An important factor in the rising accident toll is the in-
sufficiency of *autoroutes*, and French drivers are unanimous in
criticising the Government's poor record in this field compared
with Germany, Italy and even little Holland. At the end of
1964 there were only 300 miles of *autoroute*, consisting of short
stretches in the vicinity of Paris and other large cities, while there
were 1,800 miles in Germany and 850 in Italy. Under the
pressure of public opinion the construction programme has been
stepped up in France in the past few years, and by the end of
1968 there were 700 miles of *autoroute* in service. Under
the fifth plan, 120 miles should be built each year, and by 1970
the Lille-Paris-Marseilles axis should be completed and extended
soon afterwards at each end to link up with Dunkirk and Nice.
The other projects are the Normandy *autoroute* linking Paris
with Rouen, now near completion, and a more long-term Paris-

———

The modernistic architecture of the new lycée at Reims reflects
the streamlining of the educational system which has been
going on under the Fifth Republic.

Bordeaux-Spanish frontier *autoroute*. Tolls are charged on all the longer stretches, an imposition the French motorist resents all the more as he believes he pays the highest price in the world for petrol, about $1 (8s) a gallon. Motor insurance tariffs are also high compared with Britain and, although there is no road tax, a ticket must be purchased each year, costing up to $30 (£12) for a medium horse-power car. The average French motorist only drives about 6,000 miles a year.

AIR

The French take great pride in the national airline, Air France, and they have reason to do so. Although it carries somewhat less passengers and freight than its leading British and American rivals, Air France claims to have the longest network in the world—148,000 miles, serving 113 airports in 61 countries. The company was formed in 1933 by the fusion of the five main airlines of the time. The State has a seventy per cent holding, and the Government appoints the president for a six-year term. For most of its existence Air France has been granted State subsidies in return for exploiting unprofitable routes serving the overseas territories, but for the past two years the company has recorded substantial profits for its total operations.

In 1965 the company employed 24,000 persons and its fleet consisted of 260 planes, including sixty-four jets. Boeings are used for the long-distance routes and Caravelles for the European, North African and Middle East routes. Like BOAC, Air France plans to use the Anglo-French supersonic Concord, which will make the Atlantic crossing in less than three hours. In 1965 Air France carried 4.08 million passengers.

A second international but privately owned airline called the *Union des Transports Aériens* (UTA) was formed in 1963 by the merger of two existing companies. UTA complements Air France services with a far-flung network of about 120,000 miles serving forty-four airports in Africa, the Far East, Australia, Polynesia and the west coast of the United States. Both passenger and freight traffic on UTA are increasing rapidly, and over a quarter of a million passengers were carried in 1965.

After an unsuccessful attempt to establish a domestic air service in 1954, the Government tried again a few years later, and since 1960 *Air Inter* has built up a flourishing traffic between Paris and the main provincial centres such as Lyons, Bordeaux, Strasbourg, Toulouse and Marseilles. From half a million in 1964, the number of passengers carried had doubled to 1.1 million in 1966 and new links between provincial cities are being added each year.

Paris airport, which consists of Orly to the south, Le Bourget to the north and several aerodromes for light aircraft, was used by 6.6 million passengers in 1966, which makes it the fourth busiest airport in the world after New York, London and Chicago. The beautifully designed Orly has, in addition, achieved the reputation of ' the most visited monument in France ', and the record of four million sightseers in 1966 easily beat that of the Eiffel Tower. Like London, both Orly and Le Bourget are near saturation point, and work has already begun on an immense new airport called Paris-Nord which will cover an area one-third the size of Paris proper and be able to handle thirty million passengers a year by 1985. The first stage, costing $156 million (£65 million), will be in service in 1972, replacing Le Bourget. Unlike the proposed new airport for London at Stansted, Paris-Nord has aroused scarcely any protests, as it is situated in the middle of relatively uninhabited farmland. Orly is also obliged to expand, and Orly-West will be ready in 1971 for domestic and European flights. The planners, looking even further ahead, are talking about Paris III, which will probably be sited about fifty miles from the capital in the region of Rouen.

WATERWAYS

The French navigable inland waterway system is the longest in Europe, totalling 4,890 miles compared to 2,500 miles in Britain and 32,000 in the United States. The amount of cargo carried annually doubled between 1950 and 1964, when it amounted to 85.6 million tons, almost ten times the British figure.

There are about 10,000 craft in use on the canals and rivers, and since the war large-capacity steel-hulled barges of the latest design are being used extensively.

Under the influence of the Common Market, the modernisation of the inland waterway system has been concentrated on the industrial north-east corner which must compete with the neighbouring regions of the Saar and the West German and Belgian ' Black Country.' The four principal inland water routes capable of taking the new 1,500-ton ' European gauge ' barge are : the Rhine between Basle and Lauterbourg, the Moselle, recently canalised between Metz and the Rhine at Coblenz, the Seine, from Le Havre on the coast as far as Paris, and the Dunkirk-Denain canal.

Faltering progress continues to be made on the most ambitious project of all, namely the linking of the North Sea via the Rhine to the Mediterranean via the Rhône. Official government approval was given in 1962 when the project was first inscribed in the national plan, but since then only meagre credits have been allotted. Although the idea of linking the Rhine and Rhône valleys by canals goes back as far as the Romans, doubts still remain about its economic viability in view of the huge costs involved. Most of the Rhône is already navigable between Lyons and the sea, since this stretch was tamed as part of the programme of the *Compagnie Nationale du Rhône* to build a series of hydro-electric barrages along the fast-flowing river and channel off water to irrigate the agricultural land in the valley region. The big snag is to link the Saône above Lyons with Mulhouse near the Rhine and Metz on the Moselle. The existing canals, such as the *Canal de l'Est*, are unable to take barges of more than a few hundred tons, and in recent years only symbolic progress has been made on the Alsace branch between Mulhouse and Altkirch. However, a pledge has been given that some day the liaison will be completed, and perhaps by 1980 vessels with 3,000 tons of cargo will be able to sail from Marseilles up the Rhône through the heart of France to the Rhine and on to the North Sea ports.

SHIPPING

The French merchant fleet is ranked as the tenth biggest in the world, accounting for about three per cent of total tonnage. It is about a quarter the size of the U.S.A.'s and in 1965 numbered 710 ships: a gross tonnage of 4.9 million tons. The bulk of the fleet, which is largely State-owned, consists of 175 tankers, which is twice as many as there were in 1950. The number of passenger ships diminished in the same period from 82 to 53, and cargo vessels from 522 to 482.

Although total tonnage increased by one million tons over the past fifteen years, this rate was below the targets set by the national plan. For France, the effects of the world-wide shipping crisis were accentuated by the loss of her colonial empire in Indo-China and Africa, at the zenith of which Marseilles was one of the busiest ports in the world. The crisis has had its inevitable repercussions on the shipbuilding industry, where the number of workers fell from 38,000 to 25,000 in six years and several firms were forced out of business or to merge with bigger ones. Since 1961 government subsidies have been made available to the merchant marine to help it compete more effectively with its rivals, who are winning an increasingly large share of France's external trade.

Ports

The three largest ports are Marseilles, with its annexes in the industrial zone at Fos; Le Havre and Dunkirk. In 1965 about 140 million tons of cargo passed through French ports.

TRAFFIC AND PARKING PROBLEMS

With their splendid road system, it is no surprise that the French have always liked to be motorised and that firms like Citröen and Renault have sought to provide cheap but durable models like the former's ubiquitous *deux chevaux*, once described unkindly as ' an umbrella on wheels,' but tough and surprisingly comfortable for all that. In 1965 there were 197 cars for every thousand inhabitants, compared to 167 in Britain and 164 in West Germany; but the United States was far ahead with 382. Thus the number of car owners in France and other European countries has still plenty of room for expansion, a prospect which chills the hearts of the police and municipal authorities of Paris and other cities where traffic problems have reached crisis proportions. Paris, of course, is a special case.

At present the capital and its inner suburban area have 1.7 million cars, and new registrations increase by about 120,000 each year. Paris itself is regarded by the Prefecture of Police as the most highly motorised city in the world, with one car for every 3.6 inhabitants. It is hoped that saturation point has now almost been reached. A certain mystery is attached to the cars of Paris, as when all available parking space in streets and garages is taken into account there are still 220,000 cars left over. Where are they?

1970 is regarded as a magic date. By then there will be car parks able to hold over 15,000 vehicles, the expressway along the right bank of the Seine will allow motorists to traverse Paris from west to east in a quarter of an hour without being stopped by one traffic light, and the *boulevard périphérique* or ring road should be finished, permitting the entire circuit of Paris (twenty-two miles) in about half an hour. Meanwhile, Parisians must grin and bear it. There are no parking meters yet, but illicit parking is punished by a *contravention* which leads to a minimum fifteen-franc automatic fine (three dollars, 25s). About four million parking tickets are issued each year in Paris.

Suburban commuters, on average, travel shorter distances than their counterparts in London or New York, as the greater Paris region is less extensive. Most Paris commuters live in suburbs one to twelve miles distant from the *portes* or former gates of the capital which mark the administrative limits. About one in three suburban workers has a job in Paris and only two in five use cars to come to work. A comparative study made several years ago showed that far fewer Parisians use their cars for commuting than New Yorkers or Londoners, but that the percentage of Parisians walking to work was more than double that for New York and well above the figure for London. These comparisons were based on the urban as well as the suburban districts.

The large number of Parisians who walk to work reflects the inadequacy of the public transport system *intra muros*. The underground train or metro system dates from over fifty years ago, and traffic experts have noted ruefully that the present system of bus routes looks remarkably like the one in existence during the Second Empire. In addition, the first mechanical buses used on the Montparnasse—St-Germain-des-Prés route averaged 8.7 miles per hour, while today during rush hours the average is six miles per hour.

The modernisation of the transport system is being undertaken rather belatedly. It includes new and faster underground trains with more carriages and rubber tyres; a new twenty-five-mile-long metro express line crossing the capital in an east-west direction and linking the outer suburbs; a new overhead metro line between the heavily-populated suburb of Creteil and the Gare de Lyon terminus; and double-decker buses to replace the ancient but attractive single-deck buses with the open-air platform at the rear.

For a nation so passionately excited about cycling as a spectator sport, the French seem more and more reluctant to actually ride an ordinary bicycle. It is scarcely an exaggeration to say that in Paris the only people who ride bicycles are postmen and a diminishing number of policemen. A large number of students and persons who cannot afford a car use autocycles or *vélomoteurs*, but this can hardly be counted as cycling, as pedalling is limited to getting the engine started. Nowadays, of course, it takes considerable nerve to ride a bicycle in Paris, and even in the provinces the pushbike is fast becoming an anachronism; but this might explain why the *Tour de France,* the annual cycling race around France, remains such an attraction.

7

How They Amuse Themselves

THE French working day tends to be long, leaving little time over for relaxation in the evening. As school usually begins at 8 am or 8.30, the family has to be up quite early. Most factory workers are at work by 8 am also and the morning rush hour on the Paris metro is under way at 7.30. The long lunch break of one and a half to two hours means that most people work until 6 pm and as executives are expected to stay on longer the Paris peak hour traffic in the evening often reaches its worst at 7.30. By the time the long evening meal is over it is almost time for bed.

A foreigner will frequently be amazed at how early at night the French are abed.

This is only one side of the picture of course; the other is the four-week holiday now almost universal and the numerous public holidays or *jours feriés*, many of them religious in origin, which the secular republic carefully retained, such as the feasts of the Ascension, the Assumption and All Saints. May is a particularly good month for holidays. In 1967, for example, the first of May was a holiday as Labour Day, and as it fell on a Monday there was a long weekend. The following Thursday was Ascension Day and many people were able to get Friday off to *faire le pont* or bridge the gap until the weekend. A week later was Pentecost with its bank holiday Monday, and as a general strike had been called for the following Wednesday the farseeing ones took Tuesday off. November is another good month with two public holidays on the first and the eleventh for the feast of All Saints and Armistice Day.

Although *le weekend* has now passed into current French, it has not yet reached such a stage of consecration as a ' getting away from it all ' interlude as in Britain or the United States. The five-day week is becoming more general, but a large number of Frenchmen willingly give up their spare time to earn extra money, often for their annual holiday. About one quarter admit to doing *travail noir* or some profitable sideline, and almost three-quarters, according to a public opinion poll, would use a reduction in their working week to make more money rather than for leisure. The growing popularity of a weekend residence, particularly in the Paris area, proves, however, that the habit of ' escaping ' from weekday pressures is spreading. By 1970 1.5 million families are expected to have a second house in the country or by the sea, which will be three times more than in 1954. The constricting feeling of living in an apartment is undoubtedly an important factor in this social trend.

The ' great escape ' is of course the annual four and in some cases five-week paid holiday which more and more French families are enjoying. An official survey revealed that 21.5 million persons or forty-five per cent of the population went on holiday in 1966 and that the figure could be expected to increase by 600,000 each year. The sea is still the most popular place to go (forty per cent), followed by the country (thirty per cent), the mountains (fifteen per cent), and abroad (fifteen per cent).

It is a fairly recent phenomenon for the hard-to-please French holidaymaker to venture outside his beloved France for relaxation, but the habit is growing steadily though not at such a spectacular rate as some statistics seem to show. Some figures for 1965 seem to reveal that five million French tourists went to Spain and four million to Italy, but many of these were day trippers who crossed the border on excursions. However, Spain and Italy are undoubtedly attracting a growing number of French visitors, particularly the former where the lower prices compensate for the travelling expenses. The United States is still out of reach of the pockets of most people; about 60,000 French people went there in 1965. Britain, although much nearer home, is distrusted for its rain and its food, although the younger Parisians are being increasingly attracted by the mystique of 'swinging London' and Carnaby Street.

The holiday habit is quite unevenly spread, as only fifteen per cent of farmers and farm workers have one, compared with three-quarters of Parisians. The most favoured classes in this respect are, as could be expected, the executives and the liberal professions, but since 1963 virtually all industrial workers are entitled to four weeks' paid holidays and in Paris at any rate a large proportion manage to get away with their families for the full time.

About thirty-five per cent of holidaymakers spend their holiday with relatives or friends and only one in ten goes to an hotel. An increasing number take their homes with them in the form of a comfortable well-equipped tent and rent caravans. *Le camping* has become extraordinarily popular, especially in seaside areas like Brittany or the Côte d'Azur, where special sites abound furnished with sanitary facilities, shops and amusement centres. Thanks to camping, millions of people can have a fairly inexpensive holiday in some of the loveliest sea and mountain resorts in France.

There is one big flaw in the holiday idyll which is called the 'August madness' and means that a quarter of the population go on holidays at the same time, creating semi-chaos in such favoured spots as the Mediterranean coast between Marseilles and Monte Carlo, where on the most popular beaches space is limited to three square yards per person. For several years the Government made brave efforts to implement a policy of 'staggering' the annual holidays, hoping to persuade more people to go in June, July and September instead of August, but the results were very disappointing. The fault is due to the school holidays and to a larger extent to the reluctance of the bigger industries like the car manufacturers to stay open in August when supplies are difficult to assure. Paris is a deserted city in August in spite of the influx of tourists. Only strictly-enforced regulations controlling the closure of bakeries and butchers' shops have been able to assure the few residents who remain of the necessities of life.

Another holiday system which has proved almost as success-ful as camping is the well organised *colonies des vacances*, in which children of poorer parents in large cities and industrial areas can have a holiday at the sea or in the mountains while supervised by trained monitors. More than two million children spend holidays in these camps each year. They are supported by the State whose aid in 1964 was about $11 million (£4 million). Also worth a mention are the ' winter classes ' whereby 50,000 children spend a month in the Alps each year, com-bining their ordinary studies with learning to ski. Most of the expenses are paid by the local authorities of the areas in which the schools are situated and the State pays for some of the equipment.

Adults also yearn for winter holidays and a surprising number manage to get off for one or two weeks between Christmas and Easter in addition to their summer holiday. About two million people pour out of Paris alone at Christmas and Easter, provok-ing gigantic traffic jams around the principal stations. Rail trans-port is encouraged by the thirty per cent reduction offered once a year to all salaried workers, but so many Parisians wanted to benefit from the lower fares on the last weekend in July that in 1967 the privilege was withdrawn for this period.

Winter sports are available on the doorstep for the residents of Grenoble, Lyons, Nice and other large towns near the mountains, so skiing has not the ' wealthy class ' connotation that it still has in Britain for example.

One in twelve holidaymakers opt for an ' organised holiday ' in one of the special villages created by various clubs, the best known of which is the *Club Mediterranée*. The ' villages ' in Greece, Italy, Morocco, Spain, Egypt, Israel and other sunny countries are much less rigidly organised than British holiday camps, although they offer less facilities for the care of very young children.

AMUSEMENTS

A breakdown of what the French spend on amusing themselves shows that the biggest attraction still remains the ubiquitous café, crowded at midday for the end of lunch black coffee, in the early evening for the pre-dinner *apéritif*, and well-frequented at other times by the folk who like to sit, outside if it is warm enough, and watch life go by while sipping a glass of wine. Although cafés will always be indispensable features of the French scene, it has become clear that people are spending less money in them than ten years ago and that this decline can be expected to continue. The car has arisen as a formidable rival, and while the average output on cafés and cars was forty per cent and twelve per cent respectively of total spending on leisure in 1950, by 1963 the proportions were twenty-six per cent and twenty-three per cent and in 1970 were expected to be eighteen per cent and thirty-one per cent.

The French love of conversation, especially if it is witty, will probably mean that if they meet less in the cafés they will take to visiting each other more. At present one person in two claims to entertain at home or visit friends at least once a month, and an official handbook considers that this is one of the highest proportions in western Europe. Visiting in France is not the casual affair it can be in Britain or the United States where one drops in for a cup of tea or a drink. An invitation to a French home nearly always means being offered a superbly-cooked meal which the hostess will have planned perhaps weeks in advance and laboured over for several days. It would not be unusual for the meal to last three hours and be accompanied by several apéritifs, two kinds of wine, coffee and a long session of liqueurs or cognac. The guest is expected to bring along a gift such as flowers for the hostess, wine, expensive pastry or sweets.

Radio and television

As in other countries, the arrival of television brought about big changes in the leisure habits of the French. They are going less and less to the cinema and the theatre and we have already noted the diminishing popularity of the cafés, at least for passing the evening. Although less than one family in two has television its influence would be hard to exaggerate. For vast numbers the programmes of the night before form the main subject of conversation at work.

There are two channels of TV programmes, both controlled by the ORTF (*Office de la Radio et de la Télévision*) which has a monopoly of all radio and television broadcasting within France. It is under the tutelage of the Ministry of Information and is often criticised for the lack of objectivity in its news bulletins and documentary programmes. Many people would like the ORTF to be reorganised on the lines of the BBC, which has been greatly admired ever since the German occupation when it represented the voice of hope for a temporarily-vanquished France.

Channel One is intended to have as broad an appeal as possible, while the second channel, which can now be received in most areas, has a more cultural emphasis. For a person accustomed to American or British television, the French range of programmes is rather limited and clearly operates on a tighter budget. The main source of revenue is the radio and TV licences —$19 (£8) for the combined licence. Commercial publicity in the strict sense was not allowed on radio or TV until 1968, but a few minutes each day were devoted to what is called *publicité compensée,* which urges people to drink more milk, use more electricity or buy savings bonds.

The Government announced in November 1967 that it intended to authorise the ORTF to carry brand advertising. After strong opposition from Parliament, the Government still decided to go ahead.

The ORTF began colour television programmes in the autumn

of 1967, using the French developed SECAM process which has also been adopted by the Soviet Union and most eastern European countries, although rejected in western Europe in favour of the German PAL system. It is hoped, however, that a means will be devised for allowing Eurovision link-ups between the two systems.

Virtually every French home has a radio and they are extensively used, especially during the daytime when there is little or no television. The ORTF has three main channels for home consumption, a variety channel called France-Inter with France-Culture and France-Musique having similar roles to the BBC Third Programme. Most of France is also able to receive the broadcasts of the ' periphery stations ' such as Radio Luxembourg, Europe Number One, Radio Monte Carlo and Radio Andorra. To avoid infringing the ORTF monopoly, these stations have their transmitters outside the frontier but they are aimed exclusively at French audiences and have their principal studios in France. They are commercial stations with spot advertising, ·but their news coverage is first-class and their reporting of the highest quality, having the advantage of being free from the government pressures which hamper the ORTF. The commercial stations are careful not to abuse their freedom, as the French Government has substantial shareholdings in them and can make its opinions felt in various ways.

Theatre

Theatrical life in France is naturally concentrated in Paris where about fifty theatres play most of the year round. Competition from the cinema, and more recently television, has threatened the existence of a growing number of long-established houses and frequent appeals are made to the Government to ease the tax burden which is said to be one of the heaviest in the world.

Generally speaking one can class dramatic productions as being classical, popular or experimental. Four of the biggest Parisian theatres are directly subsidised by the State. The

Comédie-Française was founded in 1680 by Louis XIV and forms part of the Palais-Royal beside the Louvre. Its repertoire is mainly classical, concentrating on splendid productions of the best works of the seventeenth-century playwrights Corneille, Racine and Molière. What to a British or American theatregoer would appear as an excessively artificial and declamatory style of drama has still a strong appeal for the French, judging by the numbers who flock to see it year in and year out.

The second State theatre, the *Théatre de France,* now housed in the former Odéon beside the Luxembourg Gardens, was run by the brilliant director Jean-Louis Barrault until he was dismissed following the take-over of the theatre in the 1968 ‘ revolution.’ The repertoire is a blend of the classical and the experimental, and Barrault had braved official displeasure to produce highly controversial works. There is no theatre censorship in France, but the police have been known to ask for a play to be withdrawn if it is judged offensive to public morality.

Perhaps the most interesting of the Paris theatres is the enormous *Théatre National Populaire,* usually referred to as the TNP, housed in the modern Palais de Chaillot on the hill across the Seine from the Eiffel Tower. Specialising in the work of modern French and foreign dramatists, the TNP has tried to bring the theatre to the younger generation and the working classes. Thanks to State subsidies, prices are kept low with no such extras as tipping or expensive programmes. The actors themselves tour schools and factories to talk about their work, and as a result many people find themselves taking season tickets to see plays by Chekhov, O’Neill and O’Casey, names which before had meant nothing to them. A similar policy of reaching the non-theatregoing masses is followed by the fourth State theatre, situated in the Paris East End.

A large audience is still found to support the lighter type of drama such as bedroom comedies and farces, usually referred to as ‘ boulevard theatre ’ from the fact that most of the halls specialising in this genre are on or near the *grands boulevards,* the equivalent of New York’s Broadway. Finally there are about a dozen ‘ pocket theatres ’ promoting the *avant-garde* work of new and relatively unknown playwrights. They benefit from a limited amount of State aid.

In the provinces television contributed to the closing down of many of the long-established repertory theatres, but in recent years the Government has subsidised the setting up of national drama centres serving the various regions and of about ten permanent touring troupes based in provincial capitals. The success of this policy can be judged from the fact that provincial audiences have doubled in the past fifteen years.

The output of French playwrights in the 'sixties has not been inspiring, and the lack is reflected in the number of plays by foreign dramatists which have been produced in Paris in recent years. Plays by Pinter, Albee, Osborne and Arthur Miller have had successful runs, while the long established native authors, Achard, Billetdoux, de Montherlant and Salacrou have caused little stir with their newest offerings. Jean-Paul Sartre has virtually given up the theatre to concentrate on lecturing and philosophy. One regrettable result of the present theatrical *malaise* was the drastic curtailment of the spring international festival, the *Théatre des Nations*. It is curious to note also that recent attempts to mount musical comedies in Paris have been short-lived, the result no doubt of the change in taste wrought by television.

Cinema

In contrast to the theatre, the French cinema in recent years has shown itself to be full of creative vitality and the work of the *nouvelle vague* or 'new wave' directors is greatly admired and copied abroad. None is so prolific as Jean-Luc Godard, who can make three or four films a year on amazingly low budgets and whose more recent productions, such as *Alphaville* and *A Married Woman,* are regarded as important if somewhat mystifying experiments in the history of the cinema.

Contemporaries of Godard's like Truffaut, Demy, Vadim, Varda and Chabrol continue to make excellent films if, inevitably, the freshness and shock of their first films has been replaced by a surer professional touch. The biggest box-office successes continue to be the comedies and farces starring Bourvil, Fernandel, Belmondo, Louis de Funes, Robert Dhery and other gifted actors—not forgetting ' BB ' as Brigitte Bardot is familiarly known. Jacques Tati is in a class of his own, directing and playing the leading role in those humorous classics, *Les Vacances de M Hulot* and *Mon Oncle*.

The older generation of directors, including Robert Bresson (*Diary of a Country Priest*), H C Clouzot (*The Wages of Fear*), and René Clement (*Is Paris Burning?*) have not lost any of their earlier talent, even if their output has diminished. A cross-fertilisation of ideas between the cinema and literature is an interesting feature of recent French film-making. It has had its most notable results in the work of the young director Alain Resnais, whose collaboration with the novelists Marguerite Duras and Alain Robbe-Grillet resulted in the difficult but fascinating *Hiroshima Mon Amour* and *Last Year in Marienbad*.

On the commercial side, the cinema industry is not the flourishing business it was ten years ago. Over the past decade the annual sale of cinema tickets has fallen by forty per cent from 411 million to 233 million. In 1965 receipts totalled $176 million (£63 million) and for the first time were topped by those from radio and television licences. Until 1950 the French spent roughly the same amount on the cinema and reading matter, but today outlay on books and magazines is double that on films.

Music, opera, ballet

Statistics seem to show that sixty per cent of the French listen to music once a week at home compared to only thirty-four per cent of Italians. However it is difficult to know how much value to put on such a claim. In many cases ' listening to music ' may be no more than being conscious of a radio playing in the background. A more revealing statistic is perhaps the fact that only three per cent of the French can play a musical instrument. This figure may soon have to be revised, as the annual sale of guitars is about a quarter of a million.

France, of course, has a rich musical tradition stretching back to the seventeenth century and including such composers as Rameau, Berlioz, Fauré, Debussy, Ravel, Gounod and Bizet. In more recent times Milhaud and Pierre Boulez have achieved world-wide recognition, and the talented Maurice Jarre has become famous through his musical scores for the films *Lawrence of Arabia* and *Dr Zhivago*. In the field of *avant-garde* musical forms, Pierre Schaeffer and Pierre Henry have become known to a limited number of initiates for their experiments in ' concrete ' and ' electronic ' music. Olivier Messiaen, much of whose work is deeply religious in inspiration, is regarded as one of the most original of modern composers for his orchestral imitation of birdsong in various works.

For music lovers the principal source of music apart from their own record collections is the national radio and television network, the ORTF, which broadcasts almost 300 hours of musical programmes a week (including ' pop '), and runs four national orchestras, three choirs and several regional orchestras. The regular concerts and recitals in the ORTF's splendid new circular headquarters beside the Seine are very popular with Parisians, as are the concerts in the Salle Pleyel, the Albert Hall of Paris. In addition there are numerous private symphony and chamber music groups. Another favourite setting for musical evenings is the old St Eustache Church. Among the best known choral groups are the Paris University choir and the Little Singers of the Wooden Cross. The flourishing musical life in the provinces is reflected in the various municipal orchestras and the annual festivals in such centres as Aix-en-Provence, Strasbourg, Besançon and Bordeaux. The formation of young musicians is assured in numerous municipal academies in the provinces and in Paris by the world-famous *Conservatoire*.

The operatic tradition is maintained by the two State-subsidised lyric theatres in Paris, the *Théatre National de l'Opéra* and the *Opéra-Comique*. The former is housed in the enormous baroque-style palace designed by Garnier in 1875 and one of the best tourist landmarks after the Eiffel Tower. The repertoire is largely classical, but the critics have not been kind to the

productions of recent years although its former director, Georges
Auric, is credited with restoring some of the prestige which had
been lost since the war. The *Opéra-Comique* is passing through
a difficult period although its new director has followed the
example of the TNP in going out to seek new audiences among
the mass of factory workers and office employees, offering low-
priced season tickets for large groups. Both theatres have a
ballet corps and one night a week is usually devoted to the
ballet.

VISUAL ARTS

Paris's proud pre-war domination in painting, when no other
capital could challenge the 'city of light' as the leader of the
world in the plastic arts, did not survive the defeat of 1940 and
the occupation. Today the era of Picasso, Matisse, Kandinsky,
Mondrian, Rouault, Utrillo, Braque, Dufy, to mention only
some of the most illustrious, has passed into legend. The 'Paris
School' continues to attract many young and talented artists
still fascinated by the Impressionists, the *Fauves*, the Cubists and
the Surrealists, but the old glory of Montparnasse and Montmartre has faded and New York, London, Rome and other
capitals are challenging Paris as leaders in contemporary painting.

At the same time popular interest in the arts seems never to
have been so widespread. Exhibitions in Paris in 1967 of Picasso,
Dutch Old Masters and of Impressionists from private collections attracted enormous crowds including daily busloads from
the working-class suburbs. The exhibition of Egyptian art
treasures from the tomb of Tutankhamen had to be prolonged
by three months to accommodate the unprecedented crowds.

Apart from these 'spectaculars,' usually mounted with the
backing of the Ministry of Cultural Affairs, the numerous private
galleries in Paris run their own exhibitions throughout the year
and they are the principal channel through which the artists
reach the public and make a living. Unfortunately a crop of
sensational art forgeries, exposed recently, has thrown a certain

amount of disrepute on the modern art movement, although the dealers blame millionaire collectors for their indiscriminate demand for paintings which are not available, thus stimulating expert forgers into providing the next best thing.

Sculpture has benefited from a happy initiative by the State, which has decided that in architectural projects by the Ministry of Education such as new schools, universities and libraries, one per cent of the credits allotted will be for decorative purposes.

An interesting development in recent years has been the springing up of a series of modern art museums along the Mediterranean coast at the initiative of private benefactors. They include the Matisse museum at Nice, the Picasso museums at Antibes and Vallauris, the Cocteau museum at Menton and the Maeght Foundation at Vence devoted to Miro, Chagall, Kandinsky, Bonnard and Giacometti.

LITERATURE

In spite of their great literary heritage and pride in their language, the French are not great readers. The President, M Pompidou, who is also a distinguished man of letters, has been widely quoted as claiming that the French read five times less than the English. Disgruntled publishers complain that fifty-eight per cent of French persons over the age of twenty never open a book and contrast this lack of interest with the situation in Britain and the United States. Another statistic often put forward is that the public libraries in London lend ten books annually per inhabitant whereas the Paris libraries lend only one. However, this striking comparison may be due as much to the shortcomings of the public library system in France as to popular indifference to literature.

Thanks largely to the development of paperbacks, more books are being sold in France than ever before. 'Paperback' is a rather misleading term, as long before they appeared in Britain, French publishers were turning out cheaply-bound paper-cover books with the pages still uncut. They were normally of octavo format, however, so the handier size of foreign paperbacks quickly won favour under the name *livre de poche* or pocket-size book.

The great literary event each year is the prize-giving season in November. There are several hundred literary prizes in all, but by far the most important are the Goncourt, Femina and Renaudot. The winner of the most prestigious, the Goncourt, receives a nominal cash prize of about $10 (£4), but he or she will usually make a small fortune from the royalties of the ensuing sales which can range from 200,000 to 400,000 copies. At Christmas many people will buy the Goncourt novel automatically as a gift without having read it themselves. Naturally there is tremendous rivalry between publishers over the best prizes, but there are frequent complaints that the top three or four firms have the awards tied up as the juries are authors themselves who have strong links with the various publishing houses.

Contemporary creative writing is still influenced by the famous existentialist movement launched by Sartre in post-war Paris and whose sombre yet liberating philosophy was taken by its adepts into the cellar night clubs of St-Germain-des-Prés, the capital's literary centre. Tourists still visit them in the vain hope of reliving that epoch when the young husky-voiced Juliette Greco sang there for an anti-conformist generation in wild reaction against the constraints of four years of enemy occupation.

Existentialism as a movement is now regarded as *démodé* and discarded. Sartre himself has apparently abandoned the novel and the theatre; Albert Camus was killed in an accident in 1960 after winning the Nobel Prize at the age of forty-four, but he and Sartre had already quarrelled and parted ways; Simone de Beauvoir has devoted recent years to her autobiography.

The appearance in the fifties of the *nouveau roman* or 'new novel' characterised by an apparent incoherence and absence of plot is regarded to some extent as a reaction to the emphasis by Sartre on the necessity for the writer to be *engagé* or committed politically. The best known practitioners of this difficult form, nicknamed the 'anti-novel,' which a mystified public has for the most part ignored, are Nathalie Sarraute, Michel Butor, Alain Robbe-Grillet and Marguerite Duras.

The critical attention paid to these experiments can perhaps give the impression that there is little other worthwhile work being done by French novelists. This of course is not so, and the themes of the second world war, decolonisation and the Algerian war have been treated successfully by many novelists in recent years. A Nobel prize-winner from an older generation, François Mauriac, has abandoned the novel for journalism and his memoirs. André Malraux had temporarily sacrificed creative writing in response to General de Gaulle's call to head the new Ministry of Cultural Affairs, but André Maurois continued to produce his superb literary biographies until his death in 1967.

French poetry, the critics observe sadly, reaches a depressingly small audience, but the poets themselves are felt to be partially to blame for deliberately seeking incomprehension. The Communist poet Louis Aragon is still widely read, however, and another poet, Saint-John Perse, won the Nobel Prize in 1960. What a critic has called ' the poetry of the heart ' continues to reach the people, he says, in the songs of Georges Brassens and the unforgettable Edith Piaf.

STATE AID

State patronage of the arts and financial aid for the preservation of the country's cultural heritage has a long tradition in France. Various monarchs established national tapestry and pottery industries. Other régimes promoted the theatre, letters, music and the fine arts. The anti-clerical Third Republic passed important legislation for the safeguarding of the cathedrals and ancient monuments. The Fourth Republic was too preoccupied with the post-war recovery programme to evolve a distinctive cultural policy, but under the Fifth Republic such a policy has been energetically pursued.

From 1961 the national planning machinery has included a cultural commission and for the period of the fifth plan (1966-70)

State spending under the heading of cultural equipment will total 1,790 million francs (about $358 million, £150 million). Among the projects to benefit from these subsidies will be the restoration of historical monuments; the rebuilding of the national school of architecture and the *Conservatoire de Musique* in the Paris suburb, Défense, which is to be the centre of a 'cultural city'; increased commissions by the State and local authorities for artistic works; art exhibitions at home and abroad; low-rent lodgings for art students, and an extensive building programme for the *Maisons de la Culture* or Houses of Culture which will be described in more detail below.

Since 1959 the role of the State in the encouragement of the arts has been taken over by the new Ministry for Cultural Affairs headed for nine years by M André Malraux, the famous left-wing novelist of the thirties who later became a close collaborator of General de Gaulle. Thanks to M Malraux's vision and great prestige the work accomplished by the Ministry has been most impressive. Here only a brief summary can be given of its principal activities.

We have already seen examples of how the State finances the national and provincial theatres, but it also aids private theatres by a special fund which is used as a partial insurance against the risk of unsuccessful productions. A committee is given the task of selecting the most promising plays by writers who have never had a play produced, and the State pays the expenses of mounting them for short runs in a Paris theatre. Among the famous playwrights who have been helped in this way are Samuel Beckett, Arthur Adamov and François Billetdoux.

The film industry is largely controlled by the National Cinema Centre which, through a special fund financed by a tax on cinema tickets, advances financial aid to some of the most talented directors to make films which have received international renown. Under this scheme the directors submit their project to the centre, and if a special commission judges that it has artistic interest a subsidy is granted. This type of aid came to almost $11 million (£4 million) in 1966. If the film is a financial success further subsidies can be advanced to enable the director

to make another film. Mention should also be made of the subsidised national film school for training technicians and directors
and the *Cinémathèque Française*, which is a film museum in
Paris supported by the State. Its archives are perhaps the most
extensive in the world and the best work of French and foreign
directors can be seen in two modestly-priced cinemas throughout
the year.

Great interest abroad as well as in France has been aroused
by the *Maisons de la Culture*, first envisaged in the national plan
six years ago but which have now passed from the experimental
stage to being solidly implanted in seven regions, the final goal
being twenty-eight. These cultural centres are designed in an
original architectural style with the aim of not merely making
culture available to the less privileged classes but of encourag-
ing them to active participation. Each building has exhibition
halls, an auditorium, cinema, theatre, library, discothèque, bar-
restaurant and rooms where people can just sit and talk. Of the
eight which are already in operation, three have a professional
theatre company and all offer new dramatists the chance to stage
their work.

The centres are financed equally by the State and the local
authority. An independent cultural director is appointed, who
is free to choose his own collaborators. The State and municipal
representatives are in the minority on the administrative board.
The success of these original ventures can be judged from the
fact that in the town of Bourges, which has 63,000 inhabitants,
one person in seven is a member of the cultural centre, and the
one in the Paris East End has 20,000 members.

THE PRESS

Most French newspapers are comparatively young, dating
from the Liberation in 1944. Papers that continued under the
German occupation were considered to have collaborated and
were suppressed by the provisional post-war government, being
replaced by the numerous papers which were published secretly
by the various Resistance movements. Papers like *Le Figaro*, the

great Paris daily, were allowed to continue as they had 'sabotaged' themselves rather than collaborate.

The patriotic enthusiasm of the founders of the new press was not always reinforced by adequate financial resources and business experience and there were numerous casualties in the early years, although a sympathetic government had granted some important privileges to the press such as tax relief, low telecommunications rates, easy loans and export incentives. Today there are slightly over a hundred non-specialised dailies, including ten in Paris. Their circulations total about eleven million, about the same as the pre-war figure, and their annual turnover is estimated at about $276 million (£115 million).

Few of the Paris dailies are really 'national' in the way the London papers are. Only *France-Soir* (circulation 1.3 million), *Le Figaro* (500,000) and *Le Monde* (370,000), are read all over the country. The size of France and the difficulties of distribution are factors in the lack of penetration by the Paris dailies, but more important are the vigour and growing influence of the provincial press. Thus, of the eleven million total circulation before the war, the Paris press accounted for seven million and the provincial press for four million, but today the proportions are almost the exact opposite. The biggest regional dailies like *Ouest-France* (640,000) in Rennes, *Le Progrès* (500,000) in Lyons and *Le Provençal* in Marseilles cover so large an area that they can have between twenty and forty editions.

To a British or American newspaperman, French papers can 'look a mess' with the front page an apparent hotch-potch of headlines and pictures. On the other hand the authoritative and justly renowned *Le Monde* uses no pictures at all and thinks nothing of running an 8,000-word article on the French water supply.

The post-war press tends to be less politically committed than during the Third Republic, although the majority of dailies are hostile in varying degrees to the gaullist régime. On the other hand those with the biggest circulations such as *France-Soir* and *Parisien Libéré* support the Government. The number of party organs has diminished, only the Communist paper,

L'Humanité, having a sizeable circulation. *La Croix*, the Catholic daily, also has a large readership. A curious feature is the almost complete absence of national Sunday papers, a reflection perhaps of the French family's habit of lunching out and visiting relatives on Sunday.

On the other days of the week, however, there is an enormous audience for the flourishing periodical press, which counts no fewer than 15,000 publications, about a quarter of which can be considered as important. Political tendencies are much more marked in the weeklies, most of which are anti-gaullist. *Paris-Match* (1.2 million) has achieved world fame for the speed and quality of its illustrated reportages, making one wonder why no comparable magazine exists in Britain with its larger population. The French press does not, however, have to compete with television for advertising revenue. Another weekly, the news magazine *L'Express*, changed over to a *Time* style of reporting and presentation some years ago and boosted its circulation from 150,000 to 400,000 today.

The most profitable sections of the periodical press are the magazines devoted to women's interests, television and gossipy, wildly inaccurate stories about celebrities. In this group there are twelve periodicals with circulations of over a million. The easy-going French libel laws are taken advantage of to the full by the *presse de coeur* or romantic press which week after week literally invents stories about film stars, pop singers and royal families (especially the British) which in Britain would lead to immediate court actions and substantial damages. Another weekly to get away with murder, metaphorically, is the savagely satirical *Canard Enchainé*, but it also produces notable scoops thanks to its well-placed sources. Its treatment of General de Gaulle and ministers by cartoonists was and can be quite shocking, but such lampooning is consecrated by a long tradition in France and the victims would get little satisfaction by protesting.

SPORT

The development of sport in France on the British or

American scale has been hindered in the past by the prestige accorded to intellectual accomplishments. It is now generally accepted that the development of the body is not incompatible with the training of the intelligence, and with the active encouragement of the government through the Ministry of Youth and Sport the virtues of physical exertion for the young and the not so young are being preached.

In 1967 a 'Keep Fit' campaign was adopted as the year's national cause following the 'Keep Sober,' 'Drive Carefully' and 'Give Blood' campaigns of previous years. That the French need to be persuaded of the value of physical fitness seems to be shown from statistics which claim that only seven per cent practise some kind of sport once a week compared to twice that percentage in Britain. Many of the twenty-five per cent who say they play some sport during the year are believed to limit their exertions to the holiday period only.

At the same time there is a widespread spectator interest, frequently intense, in competitive sport. The fervour with which the accomplishments of the various national teams is followed can strike foreigners as unduly chauvinistic. Defeats for the French soccer or rugby teams are virtual catastrophes to judge by the newspaper headlines, and the referee is often made the scapegoat. This lack of sporting spirit is generally not found among the players themselves but rather among the excitable followers ignorant of the rules. The most popular game is soccer, which is played by about half a million. All sports are highly organised under sixty national federations which give licences to the members of the affiliated clubs. There are about 70,000 clubs covering all sports and their membership totalled about four million in 1965, an increase of two million since 1954.

Rugby is the great game in the south-west where the local fervour compares with that in the Welsh valleys. The imaginative, dynamic methods of the French XV have made it the most attractive and effective team in the international championship over the past decade. It is curious that Paris has only two senior sides in rugby and for the past few years no first division team in soccer, all of which seems to confirm that Parisians are not very interested in sport. In their defence it should be said that playing facilities in the capital are few, often difficult to get at and expensive to use. Golf, for example, is unknown to the vast majority; the handful of clubs in the suburbs are almost as hard to get into as the Royal Enclosure at Ascot or Burning Tree in Washington D.C. and extremely expensive.

Professionalism, with the exception of cycling, is not as widespread as in Britain. Soccer is far from being the money-spinner it is across the Channel and there are no weekly pools to stimulate interest. The annual Tour de France is the cycling event of the year, but it is also a mammoth publicity and public relations bonanza and this aspect, coupled with doping revelations, has diminished its prestige somewhat in recent years, although no other sporting event rouses the whole country to such a pitch of excitement.

The game of *boules*, also known as *pétanque*, which is a crude version of bowls traditionally associated with the Midi, has now spread throughout France and there are more registered players in Paris than in Marseilles. In the Basque country *pelota*, which has a distant resemblance to squash, is still played.

Field sports are particularly popular. About two million people are licensed to shoot, which is five times more than in Britain, and the number is growing fast although there is nothing like enough game to go round and $4 million (£1.7 million) worth has to be imported each year. Fishing is another great pastime on Sundays and during hoidays. Hunting still has aristocratic overtones and the forests of the old royal domains in the *Ile de France* are well stocked with deer.

The most favourite Sunday pastime of all is the weekly gamble called the *tiercé*. Betting on horses is only legal through the State totalisator called the PMU for short. Every Sunday an average of five million French men and women congregate in the thousands of cafés entitled to take bets for the PMU. They hand in cards on which they have marked three numbers, each one corresponding to a horse in a particular race that day. The basic stake is three francs and for the lucky few who have picked the first three horses in the right order the winning odds could be 10,000 to 1. Apart from the *tiercé*, ordinary bets can also be placed. In 1966 the French bet about $1.2 billion (£434 million). The State took almost twenty per cent, the winners seventy-seven per cent and the rest went to the improvement of racecourses and the breeding of racehorses.

Appendix

Hints for Visitors

WHEN

France has plenty to offer all tastes all the year round, but August should be avoided by those who dislike crowds and high prices. If it must be August, hotel and transport bookings should be made well in advance and confirmed.

PARIS

Here there is no difficulty about finding accommodation in August as the capital, in contrast to the seaside resorts, is practically deserted. But the swarms of fellow tourists, as well as the lack of the usual ' atmosphere,' can be depressing. September and October are the best months to see Paris, as July can be stifling and Paris in the spring, so dear to lovers, can be chilly and wet. Advantage should be taken of the excellent services of the Welcome Bureau at 7 Rue Balzac, near the top of the Champs-Elysées, which is open until midnight. The multilingual hostesses will change money, find accommodation, book hotel rooms in the provinces by telex, supply free maps, a handbook on Paris packed with information and a list of cheap restaurants. Most towns in France have a tourist bureau called a *Syndicat d'Initiative* where similar services are available.

MOTORISTS

The red Michelin guide for hotels and restaurants is, of course, invaluable and is kept carefully up to date. The Michelin road maps are also excellent and the green regional guides in English add enormously to the pleasure of visits to Paris, the Alps, Burgundy, Normandy, Brittany and the *Côte d'Azur.* Driving on the main roads in the holiday season can be nerve-racking, and if an alternative route can be planned with large-scale maps it is worth while even if some time is lost. Drivers should be careful to observe the *priorité à droite* rule, that is, give way to traffic coming from the right, unless otherwise marked. This rule applies particularly in towns at intersections where there are no traffic lights.

MONEY

France is an expensive country, especially for the tourist who cannot be expected to know all the traps. It is best to have a substantial reserve in travellers' cheques for the unexpectedly large hotel or restaurant bill. Many shops offer a twenty per cent reduction on goods bought with traveller's cheques, but because of abuses the system is to be tightened up to ensure the goods are genuinely exported.

TIPPING

A demand for *service* or *pourboire* will be made in virtually all restaurants, cinemas and theatres. The minimum expected will be ten per cent, but never give more than fifteen. In tourist areas the *service* is frequently included in the price of snacks and automatically added on to the bill for meals, but this will not always be made clear, so ask : ' *service compris?*'

MUSEUMS

Most museums and monuments are closed on a certain week-day if open on Sundays. In Paris the usual day is Tuesday.

Index